Shepherds
of the
Valley

Shepherds of the Valley

How Love Looks in Shoe Leather

To Kip - A very
Special Friend & A Super
Special Fellow - Bob Waymire (& family)

Keith Waymire

Bob Waymire
Oct '88
Old Etna

Shepherds of the Valley

ISBN 978-1-61623-190-3

Published in 2009 by Bob Waymire

Printed by Believer's Press, Minneapolis, MN

Library of Congress Cataloguing-in-Publication Data

Waymire, Bob 1930-

   Shepherds of the Valley / Bob Waymire

   ISBN 978-1-61623-190-3
      1. Wendell Seward 1925-2007; 2. Marilyn Seward (1928-
      3. Biography 4. Education 5. Pastor 6. Public Service
      7. Christian Life 8. Unconditional Love 9. Grace 10. Family Life
      11. Hospitality

Cover design: Joan French

Contents

Contents

Acknowledgements

There are several people who provided significant help in this book getting from the concept stage to the point where you now are holding it in your hand.

Dear friend, Mike Yaconelli, was very close to Wendell and Marilyn Seward. At lunch one day he and I came to the conclusion the Seward story must be told. He and I would give input, I would do research in my travels, and he had a friend he thought should do the actual writing. Mike left us later that year for a much better place…without ever mentioning his friend's name to me or his wife, Karla, or anyone else. So herein is "Plan B".

I met Kay Strom in Hyderabad, India not long after Mike's home-going. She was writing a biography about the man in whose home I was staying. "Aha!…", I thought, after learning she had written many books and was there to do a biography! The short version - Kay didn't have time to write this book, but talked me into writing it…and she would edit it. Both Kay and her husband, Dan Kline edited the book. I am deeply indebted to both of them for their kind words, and am blessed by the warm friendship we enjoy. You folks are delightfully special!

I want to thank long-time friend, Bobbie Stedman for her encouragement and manuscript reads. Her and husband Bob have been a continual encouragement and support. Bobbie's input was most helpful, as was that of her friend, Doris Rosales. I am indebted to Karla Yaconelli for her very insightful review, and for her lasting friendship that helps fill in the blank left by Mike's leaving us. Also a special thanks to Karla Gentry, near and dear neighbor, for her insights, reviews, prayers, and spiritual encouragement.

Very special thanks goes to our dearest and longtime friends, Armin and Jan McKee, who have enabled my family in many ways over the years, for providing a wonderful, quiet haven for my writing at their place in Capitola, California. And we'll still kayak to Monterey someday.

Joan (Jo-Ann) French has a special place in my heart, as does her hubby, Jerry. Joan did the beautiful artwork for the cover and typeset the manuscript. Joan and Jerry are retired printers and their landing in Etna was a wonderful boon for our valley.

The Believer's Press folks have been phenomenal and a blessing. Special thanks to Barb Lilland, 'hand-holder' par excellance, Sara Rosenberg, Aja Calhoun, and Nick Ciske for their professionalism and many courtesies…and the others that helped after this copy left my hands.

To my wife Judi, precious partner and helpmate of all helpmates! - who in a realistic sense co-authored this work - I have the deepest love, appreciation and gratitude. The contribution of her countless hours of transcription of interviews, prunings, readings, editings, encouragement and empathy are ingrained throughout.

Thanks to all of you whose testimonies are in the book. Each of you was a blessing, as was your story. It was indeed a significant privilege for me to meet each of you.

To the "shepherds" Wendell and Marilyn Seward, I can't muster the words to express the extent of appreciation I have for the impact you have had on my life, and those of thousands of others near and far. Loving and accepting us all unconditionally, and treating us so Christlike, has produced a sense of understanding as to why we exist, and how we are to live. Blessed is your Destiny!

Bob Waymire
Etna, California
August, 2009

Tributes

Luis Palau, in his book, *The Schemer and the Dreamer* (1976), says, "We know a couple in a little town called Etna in Northern California. There are only a few hundred people in Etna, but the Lord has used this couple to reach out to hundreds of people all over the western United States. We have heard testimonies of teens who had been on drugs whom God has delivered through the Seward's ministry. To me their lives have always been a tremendous example of how God can use lives totally given to Him. … Something is happening in Etna that is powerful, for the glory of God."

In April of 2001, the late Mike Yaconelli wrote… "It was 1972 and I was speaking at Mount Hermon at a pastor's conference. The subject: 'Why I don't attend church.' Young, brash, outspoken, on the edge of arrogance, I was pontificating about the ills of the organized church and explaining how churches should really function. After I finished the seminar, two middle-aged teachers approached me, explained that they were doing church just like I described and wondered if I would be interested in speaking at their church. Next thing I knew I was moving to Yreka, California, as the pastor of an almost church. The couple was Wendell and Marilyn Seward. In thirty-six years of ministry in Scott Valley, Wendell and Marilyn have quietly ministered to thousands of people all over the world from the unknown city of Etna. The Spirit of God has blessed their ministry and allowed them to make a huge impact on the Scott Valley area and beyond. Wherever Wendell and Marilyn go, they bring life, energy, hope and healing. Truly, they bring the presence of Christ and they leave His sweet fragrance wherever they go."

—Mike Yaconelli (1942-2003)

Foreword

There are some men and women who change the nature of history for the better just through the lives they live. Wendell and Marilyn Seward are such a couple. Respect and admiration for them are domiciled in thousands of hearts. No strangers to deep adversity, they serve their fellow man with humility and grace. Individuals and communities have been transformed by their unconditional love and acceptance. Many hundreds were directly touched by their hospitality and generosity. If the half were told, a shelf full of books could not contain the record. All credit is eagerly and happily given to God. They see themselves as his children, and the sheep of his pasture. Others see them as wise shepherds, lovingly caring for the flock.

They enter the registry of the saints who have laid down their lives as living sacrifices; the extent known only to God.

Introduction

"Do you like hot fudge sundaes?"

"No two ways about it!" I answered, "Glad you made it plural."

This hi-cal question was posed to my wife Judi and me in the summer of 1973 on the grounds of Mount Hermon Conference Center located among the majestic redwoods where the Santa Cruz Mountains border the Pacific Ocean. Within minutes after first meeting them, we learned Wendell and Marilyn Seward were school teachers living in a small town called Etna, California, situated in an alpine valley about four hundred miles to the north. They attended this particular family conference each year.

A half-hour later we were at Denny's, spooning ice cream and dripping fudge-y syrup. We learned that the Sewards, in addition to teaching school, also shepherded a church. Wendell was the mayor of Etna, and Marilyn was the principal of a rural school.

In those days Judi and I were with an organization[1] that held its annual family conferences at the Mt. Hermon Conference Center. The strongly outreach-minded Sewards had persuaded twenty-plus people to travel from Etna to hear the passionate speakers and musicians, and to enjoy an array of family activities, including sand sculpting on Santa Cruz Beach.

A decade and numerous hot fudge sundaes later, we would find our family of four, plus Judi's folks, "Grandma" and "Grandpa," moving to property near Etna, beginning a long era of weekly fellowship and interaction with Wendell and Marilyn that continues to this day. Judi and I remain amazed at the indefatigable energy, widespread involvement, deep compassion, warm hospitality, and fathomless love

---

1   Luis Palau Team, then with Overseas Crusades

of this unique couple. Their hearts are bigger than a Sumo wrestler's. They each served terms as mayor and a variety of roles in the public sector. The Sewards have the noble quality of seeing something worth redeeming in every person. They've seen in those whom many would say are too wicked or too worthless or too far gone, some obscure quality that, when properly nourished, blossoms and grows valuable fruit.

They have been vessels of nourishment for many such individuals, demonstrating how God's love reaches the darkest depths and the loftiest heights with redemption in its healing wings. Their seeking love finds and attracts those who are weary, downtrodden and lost, uniting them again with the Creator and Lover of their souls.

The Seward's love and home are a safe port for the weary travelers of this life. More than one hundred individuals have lived with them for six months or longer, plus thirty-six foreign students. Their compassion and servanthood, maintained by their relationship with Jesus Christ, have formed a bridge of love for many to cross from the sifting sands of their own striving to the solid ground of God's infinite grace and love.

If you are ever in Etna, take some time to visit the Seward household. You'll be received with grace and joy. And if you're hungry, Marilyn will snap her fingers and one of her famous casseroles will instantly appear…and you'll be doubly fed.

Chapter One

Is That Really You, God?

"God sees the truth, but waits."
Tolstoy

Marilyn's voice carried clearly above the noise-filled car. "At last! It's hard to believe we are finally starting the final phase of our preparation."

The couple could see their destination, Kansas City, in the distance. They were in remarkably good spirits after driving two long days in a fully packed car with two very energetic youngsters.

In reality, Marilyn and Wendell Seward had begun this journey nine years earlier when they first met at Maranatha Bible Camp in Western Nebraska. Now, nearing Gospel Missionary Union headquarters, their vision to go into the mission field was becoming a reality. Their earlier interview had gone well. They needed only to finish this next step of orientation and training before being deployed to Latin America.

For several years prior they had been occupied with envisioning, adjusting, preparing, starting a family, and saving every dime they could in preparation for this pivotal time in their lives. Both had a keen sense God had called them into full-time missionary work.

Soon after locating in their assigned living quarters where they unpacked and freshened up, the family of four, with a sense of excitement, walked across the grounds for their initial meeting with the mission leadership. The meeting, although congenial, found them a little taken aback when they were informed their field assignment had been changed from Ecuador to Morocco. This meant they would now have to learn French. It also meant they would have to use much of their savings for French lessons. Accepting the mission's rationale, and taking this surprising ripple in stride, they launched into their orientation classes and language lessons.

The mission, somehow discovering Marilyn's adroit organizational skills and abundant energy, engaged her several hours each week in a variety of tasks around the headquarters. This put pressure on the family, encroaching on time with the children and her studies, but Marilyn showed herself equal to the task.

After several weeks of study, class and office work, and working around the grounds, the day arrived for final review and field assignment. Sitting with the mission president and two others in the leadership, they were hit broadside by the totally unexpected statement, *"We're very sorry, but you are not being accepted for overseas missionary service."* No physical blow could have hurt or shocked them more. They were dumbfounded.

"We were totally speechless, stunned! How could this be? We knew there must be some mistake…some huge mistake…wasn't there? Didn't they realize our whole lives were wrapped up in this?"

"You are beyond our normal age requirement, and with your two children we feel it is best for you not to go to the mission field." Receiving no other information, they left the office in a state of shock. Too old!? At twenty four and twenty eight they were too old? Two young children were two too many! Now what?

Lord, can this really, truly be Your will? they wondered.

The mission had known their ages and family status for months. Things just didn't compute. Why would the Lord allow them to go through all those years of preparation and months of training only to be rejected? Their hearts were tuned and charged to the Great Commission to "go into all the world and make disciples…."[1] And now this!

At fifteen, Marilyn had gone to Maranatha Camp in Nebraska. There she heard a missionary speaker describe the millions of people throughout the world who were starving both physically and spiritually, because there was no one to go to be with them, to give them a message of hope, or to demonstrate God's loving care. She felt an ache in her heart. She visualized the countless children who were sick and dying and without hope, and her eyes were moist. She heard the speaker ask, "Who will go? Who will tell them?"

She began to weep softly, saying, "I will go, Lord. I will go. Help me, Lord, to know what to do. I will go!" Already known for her com-

---

1   Matthew 28:18-20

mitment and strength of character, this was no idle statement or passing emotion. That night the compass was set.

When Wendell met this young lady, he was impressed by her sense of direction and strength of conviction. He knew he could support her vision, and his own began to crystallize along the same lines.

Now, heart-broken and out on the street with their belongings, Marilyn was on the edge of despair and Wendell was numb. Nothing made sense. They were both fighting against a root of bitterness. Tough questions and imaginings hounded them day and night. "God, did we misinterpret your vision for us? Is there something you want us to learn from all this?" His answer, "Yes…there is."

They found themselves in the midst of a spiritual battle. They struggled to believe the God "who is able to keep us from falling and to make us stand before His glorious presence with great joy" was involved.

One day Marilyn said to Wendell, "I'm under conviction about the feeling of bitterness that keeps coming up in me toward that organization. It just isn't right. I need to totally forgive them…*we* need to forgive them, and ask the Lord to forgive us for not trusting Him fully."

Wendell agreed.

God does not play cruel tricks on His beloved, but He does refine them through testing. Faith helps us to understand the difference. The Sewards were growing humbler, stronger and wiser.

"It's strange how some root of bitterness kept trying to raise its ugly head," Marilyn reflects. "We would think back about how one individual, a person of authority, could set aside the life-long plan of a couple wanting to obey God's call to reach the lost. Realizing God allows only that which is good to occur for His servants, we took it as all being from His hand. Perfect peace was slow in coming, but it was coming."

Trying to discuss their situation objectively, they agreed God wasn't playing games with them and in due time would reveal His purposes. Their responsibility was to trust…and put their energy and efforts into caring for their young family: MeriJean, two, and David, four.

A memorable thing had happened at GMU. A retired missionary told Wendell, "I hope when you go to the mission field, whatever you do, that you can get with the people. When I was on the mission field we had all kinds of Bible translation and teaching, but I never led anyone to Christ. I've always felt much of my life then was wasted."

The Sewards' lives have epitomized this friend's counsel. The totality of their lives is wound up in people. Wendell later reflected, "Jesus came for people, so when something is more important than a personal relationship and helping to meet people's needs, we may be doing good things, but we're missing the substance and essence of love. I think many people are afraid they'll have to get too involved. Well, you do have to get involved. That's what it's all about."

Though the memory of the GMU experience would haunt them from time to time, they worked on walking in the Spirit of forgiveness and love. Confident the guidance would be there when needed, they determined theirs was to *be* more than to *do*. They busied themselves with things at hand: raising their young family, making a living, investing in lives, and growing closer to God.

They would later find this level of test of forgiveness would rise to the surface again.

Reflection

Forgiveness is one of the more powerful weapons in a person's spiritual arsenal. It halts resentment, bitterness, and seeking of revenge—at least on the part of the forgiver. It can defuse or prevent a potentially dangerous outcome. Loving those who mistreat and persecute you requires a super-natural attitude of forgiveness with no thought of seeing them condemned. Love is self-giving, not self-serving, and inspires hope.

Chapter Two

Pre-Shepherds

"Do not despise these small beginnings,
for the LORD *rejoices to see the work begin…"*
Zechariah 4:10a

Marilyn Reed was born at home on the family farm about seven miles from Red Oak, Iowa, on May 16, 1928. She was the first child born to Morris and Fern Reed. Within five years she would have two sisters and a brother. Twenty-two years later, another sister, Karen, would come along.

Marilyn was quite independent as a child and considered herself quite practical. She would tell her mother that sweeping the floor wasn't worthwhile if she didn't get a pan full of dirt. "What's the use?" The family was very poor, and in the first six years of Marilyn's life they lived on five or six different farms. The girls' dresses were all made from printed flour sacks. When she turned five, her mom gave her a memorable birthday party.

"We were living in a crummy little house, and Mama gave me my very first birthday party. I'll never forget the yummy pineapple Bavarian cream she made for dessert. I also got a little pair of ruffled panties. Nearby neighbors brought their kids. We had a great time.

"My dad had a real bad childhood," Marilyn recalls. "His father was very mean. When my dad would work someplace, his father would come by and pick up his paycheck. Dad only went to the eighth or ninth grade, then had to go to work. This was the beginning of the Depression years and we were very poor, living one whole year on one hundred twenty-five dollars. Our only mode of transportation was team and wagon. My mom's parents were fairly well to do and had a car. Some Saturdays they would come by and take us to Shenandoah to sell our cream and buy groceries."

"Wendell and I went back a few years ago. I caught myself remembering the swings and the old merry-go-round and the ball field, and how our teacher Miss McGinnis told us the ruts in front of the schoolhouse were those of the historic Old Oregon Trail.

"I loved books. The school library had only about twenty books, so every Saturday when we went to Shenandoah I would check out a big stack of books from the city library and read them that week, then the next week trade them for another stack. My reading really broadened my knowledge of the world. It was a wonderful way to embark on any number of adventures. The library became a very special place for me." Some decades later, she would take a leadership role in obtaining a new library in Etna, California.

Music and gardening had a front-row seat throughout her life. She loved to grow flowers in the little patch her mother gave her in the family garden. She developed a green thumb. Her mother taught her to play the piano, and she often sang with her sisters for church. She learned to sew using a treadle machine, and sewed her first dress when she was nine.

She became a Christian at ten while alone in her room after listening to the venerable Dr. Cedarholm on the radio. Her mother was a "very quiet Christian."

"I wanted so badly for my dad to become a Christian. I remember pleading with the Lord, 'Even if I have to go to hell, please save my dad.' I didn't realize until later the Apostle Paul had prayed the same thing! Dad didn't beat us kids, but he used abusive language and didn't treat Mom very well verbally.

"Later Dad did become a Christian, but was very strict and legalistic. There were no movies, no dancing, and we couldn't play Bingo even at church. Yet he would go down the road and play cards with the neighbors. I couldn't understand that. I became sassy because I thought he was a hypocrite. I wasn't a bad girl; I did mind my parents. But I was sassy when they would make an unreasonable request, like no card playing, and I was liable to say, 'Well, then why can't we play Bingo if you can play cards?' I told Dad 'I am a human being too, and I have a right to speak my own views.' It didn't do me any good, though.

"Then somehow he got hold of John R. Rice's book, *Bobbed Hair, Bossy Wives, and Women Preachers*, and this was really bad news for the family. My skirts got longer, my hair had to be worn in an 'acceptable' way, and worst of all I had to wear long stockings to school. We could listen only to 'approved' radio programs. Dad seemed to know all the rules and regulations, the law, when it came to us kids, anyway. It took him a long time to discover love and grace. Somehow we lived through it all, and over time Dad mellowed. In the meantime I often wished Dad had never become a Christian because he was so strict."

When Marilyn was a junior, she was hoping Charles Lindberg (no, not *that* Charles Lindberg) would ask her to go to the FFA Banquet with him.

"When he asked Betty Moss I was crushed. I cried and cried for days, and Dad became real concerned about me. He had heard about Maranatha Camp in Nebraska on the 'Back to the Bible' broadcast. Wanting somehow to console me, Dad scraped together the fifteen dollars for the bus ticket and five dollars for the week at camp."

Wendell Herbert Seward, born September 10, 1924, first met Marilyn Reed on the ball field at beautiful Maranatha Bible Camp near North Platte, Nebraska. It was a hot August day in 1943 when he bought fifteen-year-old Marilyn her first soft drink, an orange soda. They strolled around the grounds, finding a quiet place with a bench under a tree. This first "get acquainted" chat was mostly learning about family histories, and likes and dislikes. Later he would splurge for her first sundae. Marilyn, raised on a farm, had not tasted such delights before.

The next night her tent-mate cried most of the night. When queried by Marilyn, the girl confided that the boy she fell for the year before would hardly speak to her. Marilyn thought, *What a rogue. I'm going to stay away from that fellow.* Yeah…sure. Providence was at work. Marilyn and Wendell, "the rogue," were repeatedly seen together throughout the week, obviously enjoying one another's company.

They corresponded regularly the following year. August of '44 found them both at camp again, spending considerable time together.

"When it came time to say our good-byes," Wendell shares, "I was impressed; there was something strikingly different that separated Marilyn from the others I had promised to write to. She seemed to have some pretty firm ideas on what was important in life."

She felt comfortable in the presence of this tall farm boy and his odd sense of humor. "I really appreciated his relationship with God," she relates. "I had made the decision he was worth waiting for, hinting this to him as we were parting. But I wouldn't let Wendell kiss me goodbye. I had been reading romantic novels by Grace Livingston Hill and the heroine didn't kiss a young man until they were engaged. But my sister Dorothy said, 'you're silly...I'll kiss him.' Well, that stinker did and I cried most of the way home on the bus."

The time at Maranatha turned out to be a God thing, a *kairos* (divinely-appointed) moment for both Marilyn and Wendell. Looking back, she could see how God had orchestrated the whole thing...and it came about because of a loving father who was concerned about his daughter's sad heart.

In subsequent years at Maranatha, Marilyn played many roles: camper, counselor, and dining room supervisor. Her organizational and management skills were developed and recognized early in life. Her involvement in and to the world would steadily intensify, especially after she teamed with her husband. God is and always has been the master orchestrator of His creation, and although man challenges this with his free will, God ultimately works His will—especially through those with a heart that is right toward him. Wendell did want to be a man after God's own heart, and when he took a shine to this Iowa beauty who desired so much to be used of God to reach the lost, a partnership began forming that would be a testimony of His loving grace and power for decades to come.

Their courtship had been short and sparse. Wendell was to leave for basic training in Texas shortly after camp. Both knew there was no guarantee as to when or even *if* they would see one another again. America was at war and there was a big push against the Japanese in the Pacific. Wendell wanted to be there to do his part. It would be a long two-and-a-half years before they would see one another again.

Marilyn comments regarding her final two years of high school, "We had a lot of neighborhood parties, and sometimes a bunch of us would go into town. Some of the girls would go to movies, including my sister Dorothy, but I didn't. I just couldn't bring myself to go against my father's will.

"As a senior, I was chosen for a big part in the school play. But when Dad looked at the script and saw a fellow would be smoking a cigarette, he refused to let me be in it. The school changed the script, but Dad wouldn't change his mind. I found myself really longing for some freedom, and after I graduated it wasn't long before I had an opportunity to experience a new environment.

"I attended Chicago Evangelistic Institute at age 16, the first one in our family to ever attend a school of higher learning. I would write to Wendell somewhat regularly, but later I found it was months before he would receive my letters, and some never reached him. I would get a letter once in a while and I prayed for his safety. I sensed in his letters a sober realism, yet a very caring heart. I did find I had an interest in how the war was going that I wouldn't have had if Wendell wasn't in it. I was fond of this big farm boy, and he occupied many of my thoughts. I grew eager to see him again."

On the September day in 1924 when the doctor made a house call to the Seward farm to help in Wendell's birth, Wendell's dad was across the field putting up the final cutting of alfalfa. Their farm was near Champion in southwestern Nebraska. Wendell was the second of five children born to Leon Herbert and Lenora Steffen Seward. Wendell remembers, "I was raised in a Holiness church and went to camp meeting every year. I got saved every year at the meetings, and we had revival meetings in between. I made my real commitment to Christ just before my senior year. But all through that year I struggled with my thoughts and often felt I needed to get saved again."

He went to high school in nearby Imperial, where on a clear day, looking across the grain and hay fields, he could see objects on the horizon in Colorado and Kansas, both about thirty miles away.

"The distance from farm to school made it difficult for us kids to participate in sports because we couldn't make all the practices and games, and Dad didn't want us getting hurt and being unable to do our chores. I had to milk morning and night, and then in the summer spend a lot of time behind a team of horses, plowing. Dad got me a deferment from the draft to help on the farm, but in the fall of '43 I didn't like being left out, so I went to the draft board and told them I didn't want to be exempt any longer. It wasn't long before I was on my way to Fort Hood, Texas, for training."

"When we got on the train in Texas headed for California, the seats were all taken so I spent most of the trip standing in my own private room -- the latrine at the end of the car. By the time I found all my gear and got off the train in Oakland, my company had grouped and marched off. I felt a little silly. An MP put me with another company."

Wendell remembers clearly the day he sailed under the Golden Gate Bridge, headed for the broad Pacific and the Philippine Islands. He wondered if he would ever see the Golden Gate and home again. He also wondered about his mix-up—where would his old company end up? When later he heard they went to Okinawa where most were killed or wounded, he wondered, *Was God somehow involved in sparing me from that?* His time in the Philippines, however, was no picnic.

For sixty years, Wendell kept the story of what happened in the Philippines to himself. (It is amazing the recall a person has of this kind of experience. It is even more amazing to learn what he went through there and realize that despite the horror and savagery, his innate caring, loving self remained intact.) The following he shared at the age of eighty-one:

"As we neared the Philippines, we joined about fifty other ships and were part of a convoy. Our ship took us to Mindanao on the Zambuonga (west) side of the island. Seeing I was a big guy, they took my M-1 and give me a heavy BAR (called "bee-ay-are"—Browning Automatic Rifle—a heavy machine gun). Next they gave me magazines of belted ammunition, and an assistant to help carry the ammo and tripod.

"On our first encounter with the enemy we were way out-numbered. They were entrenched behind big mahogany and palm logs. One of our men was shot early in the fight. When it became obvious we were not going to win that day, we were ordered to retreat. I was last, guarding our rear. Alone, so to speak, I was trying to go down the hill while watching my back when some Japs jumped out to take advantage of our retreat. (They were called *Japs* when they were the enemy, otherwise they were *Japanese*.) Spotting them, I emptied a magazine of twenty rounds into that relatively small nest of men. Those who didn't fall scrambled back.

"Several of my squad hurried to my assistance, but we saw no more action that day. I was relieved when we were down the hill and safe under a cliff. I assumed we would try that hill the next day. Instead our squad was put on a landing barge that went quite a bit further up the coast, letting us off where we could see the side of the hill we were on the day before when the Japs gave us such a hard time. Sure enough, just on the other side of the river up the hill was a hut, the enemy's lookout, which commanded a view of anyone trying to scale the hill. We were able to take out the hut, and I wanted to go see if we got them all and maybe pick up a souvenir. The sarge said, 'No…we did what we came to do.' When we got to the river, the tide had gone out so we crossed and walked back to the mouth where we spent the night. Before long the rest of the company came back. When they heard our gunfire they'd stormed the hill, defeating the enemy, taking them by surprise. We had taken out their spotters.

"Another time when a patrol was sent to clean out a machine-gun nest the spotter plane had sighted, the sarge told me to stay behind since I had been going so hard and steady. He thought it would be pretty routine. I stayed back and dug a latrine. I was just settling in to a digging pattern when the patrol returned. The Japs were not as far away as they thought them to be. About an hour and a half into their patrol they were ambushed but all of the enemy were killed. We had only one casualty. Both legs of the man carrying my BAR were shattered."

One of the more memorable traumas happened one day when Wendell was leading the squad in some training exercises:

"I lifted up my rifle and pulled the trigger just as a fellow passed in front of me. Nothing happened. Later when I started to tear down my rifle for cleaning, I went faint when I saw a live round in the chamber. Why it didn't go off is still a mystery to me. The 'what ifs' have never stopped. There's just no feasible reason. It was a miracle.

"Needless to say, Marilyn was never far from my mind. I kept her letters in my shirt pocket and read many times before they got so messed up with sweat I couldn't make them out anymore. To keep awake when on watch, I fantasized about her being in the foxhole with me. I held her in such high esteem the thought of anything sexual never entered my mind.

"The first time she signed her letter, 'love, Marilyn,' my heart sure skipped a beat. She wrote saying she was going to attend Grace Bible Institute in Omaha in a few weeks and would be taking such a heavy load that she wouldn't be able to write as often. She was only writing once a month then. I wrote back, telling her she was the only person I had ever been interested in, and if she was no longer interested in me, I admired her too much to bother her any more. She never wrote to me again while I was in the service, so I never wrote her. I thought too much of her to upset her with a letter. Thus began probably the darkest period of my life.

"After MacArthur made his popular re-entry on the Philippines, my unit went into training for the invasion of Japan and I was reassigned to the engineers. I spent a lot of time in prayer in those days. I was singing in the choir at chapel, but that seemed empty as did the sermons. I did sense God was with me when I visited a prison with our company chaplain. The only female we talked to, or even saw, was a beautiful girl by herself in a separate section of the prison. She had leprosy and was a former 'Miss Philippines.' The leprosy hadn't disfigured her face or her spirit. She loved the Lord and was not afraid to talk about Him. She liked being close to the chapel as she could hear the singing and sermon.

"We took communion with the men, using one cup for everyone. Somehow, taking communion with those prisoners and knowing there was a lovely Christian girl with us in spirit made that one cup very special. It was the closest I felt to God the rest of my time overseas. I was introduced to fried bananas that evening when the chaplain and I went to the prison superintendent's home for the evening meal.

"We got to Japan shortly after the surrender on August 15, 1945. The atomic bombs on Nagasaki and Hiroshima had been strong exclamation points ending a terrible conflict! Japan was not an easy place for me, but I tried to make the most of it. I stood guard, cleared caves of gunpowder, and destroyed ammunition. I was athletic director for our company for a while and even cooked a bit.

"While on R&R[1] a Christian friend and I decided to hike up a mountain famous for its shrine. On our way up some Japanese tried to stop us. Not understanding why, we continued until we found a small shrine. On it were two small golden Buddhas. Wow! What a souvenir to take home! We each put one in our pocket. But a strange feeling came over me and I put mine back and then so did my friend. After we were down the hill a little way, we both admitted having an intensely strong feeling and thought it was something demonic. I think now it was a check from the Holy Spirit telling us we were transgressing something sacred to others. In any event, I was never again tempted to take even the smallest trinket.

---

1   Rest and Recuperation (or "Rest and Relaxation")

"When it was my time to go back to the States, I was not excited to go. I hadn't written to anyone for months, including my parents. If home was as empty as it now seemed, I figured at least I could reenlist within thirty days and continue as a sergeant. However, when I got aboard the ship headed home, things began to change. I met three other Christians and we spent most of our time together. I began to think maybe God had something for me to do even if I wasn't married. I knew I didn't want to farm. So I was stuck as to what it could be. Marilyn was more on my mind than she had been for a while.

"It was August of '46 when I arrived in the States. While walking the streets of San Francisco, I got a strong urge to call Marilyn. If she didn't want to talk to me, I knew she would be nice enough to let me know in a kind way. Well, that call was the turning point in my life. It seems since then things have just fallen into place. It was not always the way I wanted, but looking back, every turn was divinely guided."

It was sometime later that Wendell found out Marilyn had never received the letter in which he said he could no longer write to her as a friend, that he had deeper feelings for her than that. Who knows whether anything different might have happened if she received it?

Reflection

Life is existential…and it isn't. Yes, the moment-by-moment, step-by-step decisions we make, coupled with our circumstances, determine the paths we tread. Yet…not totally! The foundation for these decisions is our value system, our vision, our dream, and our belief. These develop over time. What we do reflects our character. Our character reflects where our hope lies.

Chapter Three

Foundation Stones

"What therefore God has joined together let no man put asunder."
Mathew 19:6

"I was in the girls' dorm at Grace Bible School when I heard someone running down the long hall calling my name. 'Marilyn, Marilyn, there's a long distance call for you…it's a *man!*' I rushed to the phone and was excited to recognize Wendell's voice on the other end. Wendell asked if I would be willing to see him and go on a date. I didn't even really think, I just said, 'Yes.' …however, it would be three long months before we would actually see one another. Wendell set something up with his brother and I was to meet them in Lincoln, Nebraska. I would arrive by bus and was to wait for them at the bus station.

"So in November (1946) I got permission from the school to take the bus to Lincoln for the weekend. I arrived at the bus station as planned and waited and waited, but Wendell didn't show up. After nearly two hours, being very disappointed, I decided I'd best take the next bus back. But then he arrived with his brother and sister-in-law, explaining that they had been delayed by an accident.

"Wendell and I spent the afternoon walking all around town, climbing the stairs to the top of the capitol building, enjoying the view of the city and getting reacquainted. We were waiting to attend a football game between his favorite team—the Nebraska Cornhuskers—and Indiana. It wasn't exactly the romantic evening I had in mind. We sat in wooden folding chairs right near the sidelines. He became so excited during the game he started pounding on the chair and it broke into pieces! I was so embarrassed I wanted to climb under my own chair. What happened to the mild-mannered man I had fallen for?"

Marilyn's parents drove from Shenandoah to Lincoln to pick up Wendell and Marilyn and take them both back to the farm for the remainder of the weekend so they all could get better acquainted. Wendell accompanied Marilyn back to Grace to begin his Bible training at the start of a semester in January of 1947. Later in March, Wendell popped the question. Marilyn shares the memory:

"We were sitting on a log in Elmwood Park, when Wendell proposed. I had sensed that he might do this, and I still couldn't guess how I was going to act. But as soon as he asked if I would marry him, I said, 'Yes,' and then he finally kissed me, and this time I didn't try to stop him. I had an excitement in my heart and I knew right then I was doing the right thing ... although I've had plenty of times for a little doubt after that!" Marilyn quips.

"I graduated from Grace on May 25, 1947. My last semester, I took twenty-six hours of classes, had two jobs, and took voice lessons. I was so beat by the time of graduation, I slept through famous Henry Ironside's commencement address. A week later, on June 1, 1947, we were married in Shenandoah. Mrs. Carstensen, whose husband performed the wedding, gave us a card containing three dollars and a note saying, 'Use this for a dinner out when you need it,' and the verse, *As thy days, so shall thy strength be.*[1] I have used this same verse in cards to newlyweds many times, but the three dollars has inflated, of course. The next day we started pastoring Cedar Creek Berean Church in the sandhills, twenty-three miles north of Burwell, Nebraska.

"At our first service at Cedar Creek there were eleven people. It wasn't long before the church grew to about seventy-five, mostly from farms and ranches." Marilyn was nineteen and Wendell, twenty-three. "They called us 'the kids.' We had no electricity, but a small gas-powered generator (hard as the dickens to start) provided lights for the church and our little four- room house...with an outhouse over the hill.

"After about a year the men of the church put in a well on the hill behind the house. A windmill pumped the water into a tank that gravity-fed the house. The cooler was a barrel buried in the ground filled with water, which kept marginally cool. I cooked on a three-burner kerosene stove and had a small portable oven that sat on two of the burners. Our salary from the church was one hundred forty dollars a

---

1   Dueteronomy 33:25

month, and we had a seventy-dollar car payment. If we were going to stay past the summer, I (Marilyn) had to get a job.

"We were hardly settled in when we invited a young couple for dinner one Sunday to get better acquainted with people our age. I put a small roast in the Presto cooker, but misread the instructions. Well…I ended up with this little crispy-burnt sacrifice. Agonizing over that and trying to think what in the world I could fix, another catastrophe struck. I had fixed my first jello salad containing tomatoes and cucumbers. I remember mom would place the jello mold in hot water, but I didn't remember for how long, so I ended up with jello soup. We sat down to canned salmon and boiled potatoes, and that was our whole dinner. I finally confessed my boo-boo and we all had a good laugh, and we seemed to have a special bond after that."

In the fall, Marilyn began teaching and janitoring at a one-room school of twenty students, which paid a hundred and twenty-five dollars a month. She rode a bicycle to school until they bought an old pickup. Wendell started his college education under the GI Bill, enrolling in York College located in York, Nebraska, about one hundred fifty miles distant. He was leaning toward studying for a pastorate, but at this point was getting his general education requirements out of the way.

During the week while Wendell was away, Carolyn, a sixteen-year-old teacher from another country school lived with Marilyn. (This was their first "live-in" teenager. There would be many dozens more.) One night, a bolt of lightning struck their chimney, crumbling bricks and dancing across the iron bedstead they were sleeping on! From then on, every time a lightning storm would appear in the distance they steered clear of the bed!

Rowena Freeland, one of Marilyn's students, came from a family living in abject poverty. Her parents were harsh and often cruel. She had no decent shoes and hardly anything to eat at lunch time. Fifty-seven years later, Marilyn heard the "rest of the story." Rowena is seventy-two at this writing, only six years younger than Marilyn. They had lost track of each other. Then, through a mutual friend the contact was made, and Rowena came to Etna. It wasn't until a few months later when Judi and I visited her in her home in Wilhoit, Arizona, that we began to understand the significance of her visit:

"I was living in Amelia, Nebraska. Marilyn was teaching her first year. She was nineteen. I had just turned thirteen. My sister and I went to school together and in winter it was terribly cold and our clothes were so thin. Our family was very poor. When it was bitter cold, below zero, Marilyn would drive her old truck to our house to pick us up. Otherwise we'd run a quarter-mile to the road and she'd give us a ride. She saw my sister and I had only parched corn to eat for lunch, and just real thin clothes, so she started making hot soup on Fridays for the whole school and she gave me a sweater. We were used to being hungry, but I think it hurt her to see us that way. She and Wendell were poor too.

"I felt singled out and special to her because she showed me special attention, teaching me to ride her bike and to type. She made such an indelible mark on me because of her love. She's the first person I can remember who smiled at me. There wasn't anything I could do that wasn't the right thing. I remember how Marilyn always had a lot of energy. She has a ton of common sense. You know how happy she is; she was always happy and made us feel happy. She had a tremendous impact on my life. Her love is something I've cherished and has given me hope all these years, and I've tried to pass it on. It's funny how love does that."

Rowena Freeland, a tributary stemming from Marilyn's loving care, now collects and distributes clothing and food for the less fortunate and tutors people with learning disabilities.

"We had been at Cedar Creek a year and a half when our son David was born in a hospital in Burwell, Nebraska, October 5, 1948. We had saved up a little bit of money to pay for the baby, but when we went to pay the bill, the nurse, after checking with the doctor said, 'That bill has been taken care of. You have no bill to pay.' We were flabbergasted—what a blessing to us. We used the money to buy a stove.

"David was five days old when I plunked him on the front seat of the church while I played the piano at our mission conference. Our doctor was there. I remember he gave a hundred-dollar offering. We were just awed! That was a huge amount then. Years later we heard he had become a Christian."

Wendell and Marilyn's initial three-month summer commitment to Cedar Creek turned into an enjoyable eighteen months. They had made many friends, especially Marilyn, between the church and her students at school, and it was tempting to stay on at Cedar Creek. However, their commitment to the foreign mission field predated even their marriage, and since Wendell had finished the year at York, they felt it was time to move on. In the early fall of 1948, when Wendell learned he had been accepted at Baylor University in Waco, Texas (he had sent an application shortly after enrolling in York), they gave their notice at Cedar Creek. Baylor had been on Wendell's radar screen since his basic training in Texas.

This was a time of many mixed emotions, but also of significance. Leaving the newly made friends in both church and school was not easy. Yet, they knew if they were going to be ready for the mission field, further education and preparation was necessary, and soon.

These first eighteen months of the Sewards' married life were significant in that some meaningful adjusting took place, and foundation stones were being laid that would be important to their later lives.

One stone was *hospitality*. Although their initial experience of having friends over turned out to be slightly frustrating, and undoubtedly smoky…at least it turned out. Getting into tizzies because the house isn't spotless and the food isn't perfect can do damage to both the hospitality *and* the emotional state of the person offering the hospitality.

And…they had taken a girl in to live with them. This involves more than just a "gifting." It requires a certain sacrifice and willing vulnerability—to make room in your home, thoughts and schedule for another—to give up a piece of your privacy, opening yourself up to others.[2]

Another foundation stone was their *teaching*, both in school and the church. This was an area of gifting, but also required consistency and commitment. A particular characteristic taking form was their desire to impart to each child and person that they were valuable in God's sight, and to help them have a foundation in their lives toward becoming fulfilled in the role God had created them for.

A wide spectrum of adjustments are required if a marriage is to be successful. When personalities differ as much as this couples', the adjustment takes a strong commitment emanating from love…as love does not seek its own way.

---

2   During their lifetime they would host in their home over a hundred people who lived with them six months or longer. Sometimes this included mother and child. Additionally, they hosted thirty-six foreign students, each of whom stayed for a school year.

Reflection

Love plays the pivotal role in a truly God-honoring relationship. Love and respect for one another form the basis for mutual understanding and mutual submission. In these areas, the early signs were positive. Long term vision and commitment can keep us focused while an attitude of mutual re-enforcement is developing.

Chapter Four

Transition

---

*"Faith urges the believer onwards so that he
cannot settle at ease in the world."*
Soren Kierkegaard 1813-1855.

It was the winter of the great blizzard that covered much of the central and western states, when at Christmas break 1948 Wendell braved the long drive north to pick up his family. He had started at Baylor University in November while Marilyn and young David stayed back in Cedar Creek to wrap things up and pack their meager belongings.

With Marilyn's dad, who was helping them move, they began the challenging trip back to Waco. The roads were icy and the drifts were as deep as ten feet. A late night blowout sent them hunting for a tire. Marilyn's dad walked until he found a farmhouse. She explains,

"Hearing our dilemma, the farmer handed Dad the keys to his truck and gave him directions to the nearest tire shop. The generosity and trust of that farmer in total strangers made a lasting impression on us. We wanted to pass it forward."

Finally arriving safely—and tired—in Waco, Marilyn settled the family into a campus apartment and Wendell continued his studies. Wendell used the G.I. Bill to help with his college bills; however, they both needed to work to cover living expenses. Marilyn landed a well paying civil service position at nearby Connelly Air Force Base. Wendell divided his time between full-time studies and working.

He changed majors from Religion to Education when he found he didn't agree with some of the doctrines the school taught. In time, this change of major would prove providential. During the second year at Waco, the Sewards shepherded a Baptist church in a small town thirty-five miles northeast of Waco. That year they welcomed their second live-in teenager, Jeannie, into their home. She needed a place to live while working in Waco.

Baylor accepted Wendell's credits from York and he received his Bachelor's degree in August of 1951. Planning ahead he had inquired about the one year "Grad Course" at Multnomah School of the Bible in Portland, Oregon, and was looking forward to attending in order to reinforce his biblical knowledge and application. They were expecting their second child in early August, just nine days before they were scheduled to leave. On August sixth, Jeannie drove Marilyn to the hospital and little MeriJean made a quick entrance. By the time Wendell arrived from work it was all over.

"Our first stop on the long trip west was to Iowa to surprise my family," Marilyn says, "with their new granddaughter whose arrival we wanted to keep a secret for some now-obscure reason. After seven weeks of over one-hundred-degree weather in Waco, we were looking forward to cooler Oregon, and we ended up loving the fresh green of the Northwest."

In Portland they rented an apartment and Wendell enrolled at Multnomah. Marilyn was able to transfer her Texas Air Force experience to the Portland Air Force Reserve Training Center.

With Marilyn working and Wendell going to school plus working, someone was needed to take care of the two youngsters. This fell to Wendell's parents, a hired baby-sitter, and from time to time, the landlady of their apartment. (Four years earlier Wendell's parents had moved west and were in Portland. This turned out to be a real blessing.) Wendell had found a job at a service station with an attached parking lot, and it wasn't long before he was evening manager of both. This often put him home quite late—1 to 2 a.m.

Wendell enjoyed his classes at Multnomah. However because of his work schedule it wasn't uncommon for him to doze off in class. When someone would start to awaken him, Dr. Mitchell[1] would say, "Just let him sleep. He needs the rest." Wendell remembered something Dr. Mitchell shared with married couples in the Grad Class, "Sometimes in married life it's more important to bring home roses or flowers to your wife than to put an extra piece of bread on the table, because relationships are more important than your stomach." That rang a bell with Wendell.

---

1   Dr. John Mitchell was Multnomah School of the Bible's founder and an outstanding Bible scholar. He and Wendell developed a lasting friendship.

He says, "Well, I did bring home a few potted plants because I thought they lasted longer. But now, when Marilyn goes on trips I always try to have roses waiting for her when she returns." The last time Wendell and I went to the airport to meet our wives, Wendell remembered the roses.

"The summer after I graduated from Multnomah," Wendell relates, "the pastor and now dear friend, Herbert Anderson, of Gladstone Baptist where we were attending, was taking the summer off for studies, and asked me if I would take responsibility for the pulpit and 'marrying and burying.' I admired him because he was so accepting of all people. During that summer, I invited Mark Hatfield to speak. He was at that time running for Secretary of State for Oregon.

"One of Hatfield's remarks has stuck with me: 'For the Christian man to reason that God does not want him involved in politics because there are too many evil men in government is as insensitive as for a Christian doctor to turn his back on an epidemic because there are too many germs there.' He later became a US senator and was known (and persecuted) for his non-compromising stance when it came to ethical and moral integrity. He put God above organized religion and politics.

"Hatfield was one of the finest Christian men I have ever met. If it hadn't been for men like Mitchell and Anderson and Hatfield, I probably wouldn't have the perspectives I have on the value of people and the minimizing of differences. The perspectives of these men made it possible for me to later understand Mike Yaconelli's revolutionary message on freedom versus religiosity. I feel I owe a lot of my thinking today to those fellows."

It wasn't long after Wendell had received his certificate from Multnomah on June 1, 1952, that they began their missionary training for an overseas post. Then, as we saw in Chapter 1, after months of training for cross-cultural overseas service they were abruptly dismissed by the mission agency with an explanation that left them guessing. Although at the time their disappointment was beyond words, their close relationship and commitment to the Lord gave them the faith to believe God was at work, and they would trust Him with the days ahead.

They found themselves "out on the street" with hardly any funds, having spent the limited amount they had on French lessons and other expenses not covered by the mission organization. With their two kids they headed for Iowa where Marilyn would live with her folks for the summer. Wendell would go on to Omaha and take a job as a taxi driver.

He reflects, "During the three months I drove a cab, I received quite a liberal education. My cab clients ranged from self-educated philosophers, to artists and sports personalities, to ladies of the night hopping from hotel to hotel. Like the job at the service station and parking lot, this kept me in touch with the way the world lived and thought. Later, I realized both experiences were important schools."

They finally decided to go back to Portland and there things seemed to miraculously tumble into place. Wendell was able to return to his old job at the parking lot and service station, and they moved back into the same house with the same landlady. Soon Marilyn was again working at the airbase. It had been eight and a half months since they had left. Coming down the "pike" were a whole new set of circumstances that would set a new course in their lives.

Reflection

There are people and events in our life that help mold who we are. And, suffering plays its part. It comes with the territory. God designed it that way, and it is a vital part of character building. Disappointments, and how we handle them, mold...and reveal...our character. Wendell and Marilyn, finding themselves amidst various challenges and trials, were beginning to internalize the reality of the Apostle Paul's declaration, "... we are not adequate...(in) ourselves...our adequacy is from God."[2]

---

2   The Apostle Paul realized that *in and of himself he was highly qualified to be utterly useless.* See 2 Corinthians 3:5 and Philippians 3:8.

Chapter Five

Out of the Wilderness

*"One of the hardest things in life we have to learn
is which bridges to cross and which ones to burn."*

The beautiful City of Roses—Portland, Oregon—straddles the Willamette River that pours into the mighty Columbia at the city's edge. The Portland area became a place of healing and reorientation for the Sewards after their traumatic experience in Kansas City. Wendell landed a job teaching seventh and eighth grades the next fall, and left the service station. Marilyn's work at the airbase was going well.

"I worked with a real rough and tough lady, but we got to be good friends. I still have her fudge recipe that I use every year. She became very ill with an enlarged heart and I visited and prayed with her regularly in the hospital. I can remember her saying, 'You know, it's a shame that I had to wait till I was way down before I looked up to God. But, I guess that's why He's there for us.'" She died shortly afterward.

In 1956 they bought their first house, in Clackamas, about fifteen miles from central Portland. "We paid $5700 for an old house with a wonderful yard, holly trees, and a big swing. It was a great place for the kids to play. I even had space for a garden."

The move placed them closer to church and the kids' school. Marilyn juggled work with a demanding schedule, caring for the kids, sewing clothes, all the home-making chores, and planting and caring for the garden. Summer's added activities now included canning along with taking the kids to the beach. Wendell's work kept him hustling. They were getting more involved with Gladstone Church, and periodically Wendell taught in several different rural churches. Pastoring and teaching, sharing, caring and parenting filled up all the niches of time when they were not working their Monday-through-Friday jobs. This pretty much characterizes most of their married life. Marilyn happily accepted an offer to teach in Shubel Elementary, quitting her job at the air base.

In 1957 they were invited to pastor a church in nearby Colton. Marilyn shares, "In June we made the move to Colton. We put the Clackamas house up for sale, which tugged at my heart more than a little, because the new church had only a small four-room-plus-bath parsonage. That fall I started teaching at Colton Elementary. As it turned out we spent five years in the little parsonage and it *was* convenient to the school where David and MeriJean attended."

Wendell and Marilyn were developing a pattern that was to continue for the balance of their lives. They found themselves with wall-to-wall activities in the community. Marilyn was active in the PTA, Garden Club, and in hosting home Bible studies. She loved music and had purchased a Hammond Extra-Voice organ with an early school paycheck. She organized and led a choir, and one of their first challenges was putting on a cantata, *Night of Miracles*. Wendell attended the Rotary Club periodically, was active in a pastoral fellowship, and attended the kids' sports activities whenever possible. He looked for ways to be with people from all walks of life.

Nineteen sixty-two saw them moving onto "the farm": seven acres on a high hill overlooking Colton. It came with a sizeable old "very unmodern" farmhouse, and various outbuildings including a big barn. Marilyn was thrilled with the large orchard of cherries, apples, plums and pears, and the old-fashioned well house. Canning was going to be a major operation. Generous portions of elbow grease, cement, wiring, and plumbing were invested in a new bathroom, sewage system, kitchen cabinets, and so on. Their reward was a beautiful view of Mount Hood and green valleys in every direction. Marilyn writing to friends said, "In our hilltop home above Colton I even have an old-fashioned wood cook-stove in the kitchen, and I cooked Christmas breakfast on it! It was so like the Iowa farmhouse where I grew up."

When David was fourteen and a freshman, he joined the Continentals, a new quick-rising Christian singing group sponsored by Portland Youth for Christ. He enjoyed the concert tours which included traversing the Pacific Coast. MeriJean, eleven, was beginning the seventh grade. She was enjoying her youth group and school. However, she did resent her mother not allowing her to have the nice shorter-length dresses that all her friends were wearing. (Mom apparently had a short memory about her own experience with this. It's funny how that works.)

They had been at the church in Colton a little over five years when a church board member showed up at Marilyn's school one day. With little preamble he told her they wanted them to leave the church. This also caught Wendell cold, and threw the couple completely off balance. When the congregation got wind of this, they were upset and immediately overrode the board member, who thought the Sewards were departing too much from their denominational traditions. (Old wineskins *are* comfortable…but rigid.[1]) The upshot was that the board member left. From that point on the church grew at a good clip, and they began a vigorous missions program. In the coming years the Sewards would be known for "doing church" in a non-rigid way…new wineskins for new wine.

Marilyn reflects on the difficult days in her annual newsletter: "Satan has buffeted us from every direction. After these many months, there does seem to be peace and light ahead. We have marveled at the Lord's doing; even in the midst of our problems, He has brought to Himself those 'who were being saved.'" (Acts 2:47 NASB)

Reflection

Showing—*giving*—unconditional love and acceptance is a tough challenge, requiring self-sacrifice. Wendell's living "the greatest of these is love" would occasionally get him into trouble … which put him in very good company.

"In the fall of 1964 I decided I would take off a year from teaching and enroll in Portland State to pursue a long overdue Bachelor's degree," Marilyn recalls. "I had been teaching since the forties with a temporary credential, and not even that when I began in Nebraska. It was

---

1   Traditional structures (like old stiff wineskins) are often too rigid to adapt to new and more appropriate conditions and situations (new wine). Jesus uses this illustration (Matthew 9:17, Luke 5:37, 38) denoting the "new wine" of the new arrangement for living (the New Covenant) He was sharing cannot be contained in the rigid rules and laws of the Pharisees (the Old Covenant).

becoming more obvious teaching would, in all likelihood, be an ongoing part of my life. Well, I can't believe I did it, but I wanted to finish in one year so I took *sixty* units! The family had to pretty much fend for themselves. MeriJean made it possible by fixing most of the meals and running the house."

Over the years, Marilyn's stamina and pace became legendary, many claiming she could outdo the Energizer Bunny. Now approaching fourscore, her eye is not dim, nor vigor abated. She and Wendell were getting into a pattern of pouring a large portion of their earnings back into the needs of the community, church programs, and individuals. They stayed up on the latest in education and the Christian mission. Periodically, over the next twenty-five years, the two of them would take courses,[2] attend conferences, workshops and seminars, and read contemporary works to help them become and stay effective salt and light in society.

Marilyn, a book-lover who reads a broad spectrum of novels, adventure, biographies, literature classics, Christian life, and mission-related works, avidly encourages everyone to take advantage of the tremendous resources books afford. She believes every avenue in life can be enriched by reading good books,

The Sixties were stressful and painful for those serious about their Christian beliefs. The Sewards were not immune to these concerns. The presiding culture was spawning an increase of family problems and invading the Church more than the other way around. The Supreme Court became an ally to several humanistic paradigms, condoning abortion and restricting prayer and freedom of religious expression. Wendell and Marilyn felt most religious approaches to the cultural upheavals weren't very helpful.

Marilyn reflected upon her concerns, "This year has seemed rather different in some ways. When the statisticians tell us that there is no evidence that Sunday school attendance or Bible knowledge has any effect on behavior—and this seems to be verified by what we see everywhere—then we must evaluate what we are doing. Churches seem to focus mainly on Christians inside their walls and teaching them more doctrine, but they aren't very sensitive to the criticism launched against them by those seeking for love, truth and reality, who often find churches judgmental and repelling. How can we reach people

---

2   Marilyn received her Masters in Education in 1982.

with Christ's love if we keep focusing on their problems? Today's culture is saturated with teenagers searching for real meaning to life, and many are rejected because they don't fit the mold."

It pained the Sewards to see so many homes, Christian and non-Christian, experiencing serious troubles, especially separation and divorce. "At times," Marilyn states, "I feel the work we're doing is not producing many positive results in families and the community. People are self-centered, or even church-centered, but not Jesus-centered. We know God's love has power to transform lives and families if those who have His spirit will live out this love to all people. Love must be a lifestyle, not just a creed. This requires the Holy Spirit having His way in people's lives. That's what being a disciple is all about. We're convinced the Church, the family of God, needs to have a deeper and more intimate relationship with the head, Jesus. Only He has the power to change lives so they align with righteousness. Only then will there be any significant and lasting, positive change in society. So we keep asking ourselves, how can we make our work more effective? What do we do…what should we do…that will pay off in consistent results? How can we truly become more effective salt and light?"

They realized this wasn't just a local problem but a world-wide one for the Church. It dawned on them that they would have to focus on their own territory, although their concern was for the whole world. They would act upon whatever God put in front of them. As the saying goes, they were "thinking globally, and acting locally." At year's end (December 1965) in her annual newsletter, Marilyn states, "One thing I know: the world demands a consistent standard of behavior from Christians. Will you pray with us that our own conduct will be pleasing to God and to men, that the chief witness we give will be that Jesus Christ can change lives, including ours? People must be our focus. Loving, serving, helping and accepting them no matter who they are. Jesus has to become radical in our lives to make this happen. We all need to be shaken from our comfort zones!"

A year later Marilyn was still relating their consciousness of ever-present needs. "We cast longing glances at overseas teaching posts, and short-term missionary openings. The need for three thousand foster homes in this immediate area causes us to feel a responsibility here too, with our big barn, yard and house."

Over the next forty years those longings would develop into actions that touched thousands of lives all around the world. At this point, they were teaching, raising a family, and had many responsibilities, including pastoring. Little by little the salt left the shaker, flavoring society and arresting corruption, and the light of truth shone brighter, and those hidden in darkness came into the marvelous light. Their orchard and garden brought a bountiful harvest—and—the harvest of the Kingdom of God was also steadily growing. God was showing His wisdom and strength in their times of frustration and weakness. The humility and purity of their hearts was raw material He could work with.

David, then a senior, surprised them when he said at supper one evening he was asking Governor Mark Hatfield to be their graduation speaker. Having been asked to make the arrangements for the speaker, he said jokingly to his friends, "Well, the president is probably already spoken for, so I'm going to contact the governor." Sure you are! "Well, I got to thinking about it and thought it won't do any harm to ask, so I wrote him." Governor Hatfield replied he would be delighted to speak! David became a hero overnight. When the word got out, the place was packed—the largest crowd ever to squeeze into Colton High's gymnasium. Several years later Wendell remembered, "I was in Washington, DC, for a presidential prayer breakfast and looked up then-Senator Hatfield. He remembered the Colton occasion well, and asked after our son."

"There's school, then there's the church," Marilyn wrote. "We never know which comes first, honestly. March '66 will make nine years for us here at Colton. Sometimes we feel our work is finished here; other times we see no way clear to leave. We tend to be self-satisfied and complacent and we don't want this to be our lot. Yet in admitting this, we tremble a little …for at times the Lord uses stringent measures to shake us out of this." These stirrings in their spirits were harbingers of a process about to begin. The dangerous Jesus heard their hearts.[3]

---

3   Jesus, always on the offensive to bring us into the relationship of His love and on to maturity, is dangerous to our comfortable and self-indulging ways. He is quick to spot a spark of honest desire and fan it into flame; sometimes purifying and painful; in the end always warming and rewarding.

In early summer of 1966, Wendell attended a pastor's conference at Hume Lake, California, near the giant Sequoias. Marilyn went along for a break, but since the conference was men-only, Wendell had to smuggle Marilyn in; she stayed in separate quarters. At the bath house she met a woman from Yreka, California, who, surprisingly, was a friend of Marilyn's former bridesmaid. She told her that her bridesmaid, whom Marilyn had lost track of, was now married and, quite surprisingly, living in Yreka. On the way home, the Sewards stopped in Yreka, renewing their friendship with the Sandens who were pastoring the Berean church.

Marilyn fills in the story. "We had been sensing God was telling us our time in Colton was coming to a close. Not long after returning to Colton, and as the result of a 'chance' meeting with an old friend, we received an invitation to start a new church signed by three couples from Etna, a small town located in a valley twenty-six miles from Yreka. The couples had been driving over the mountain to Yreka and were attending the Berean church. The Sandens suggested they contact us as we had mentioned to them we thought God was telling us a change was coming. We made another trip to investigate."

The upshot of all of this was, on July 26 of 1967, Marilyn, now thirty-nine, wrote to the Colton church family and friends, "After ten years at Colton we will now serve with a newly organized church in Scott Valley[4] of Northern California. The first Sunday in August we will begin services with the Scott Valley Berean Fundamental Church in Etna, California. It has been a hectic but delightful summer, getting ready to move, let me tell you. We certainly are filled with mixed emotions but definitely feel God is leading us into a new era in our lives and in yours. We believe the change will be positive for everyone."

They departed the Portland area with their hearts and lives touched and molded by many friends and experiences. Yet in their own household there was a teenage girl who was anything but excited about the move.

Reflection

Change can be threatening. The elements of the unknown can be foreboding, and, obtaining consensus plus leaving old friends and famil-

---

4   Not to be confused with Scotts Valley located among the redwoods near Pacific Ocean in the area of Santa Cruz, California.

iar surroundings is very difficult. But as the saying goes, "there is no progress without change." In the Seward's situation they felt a time of change was "in the air." There was a restlessness; an unction of revelation. And when God is involved, He will provide the way to fulfill His plan. Wendell and Marilyn were sensitive to God's spirit. Like iron filings on a piece of paper that follow the moving of the magnet…when it (God's spirit) moved, they responded.

Chapter Six

New Beginnings

"We must become the change we want to see."
Mahatma Gandhi

The three Etna couples who signed the invitation offered Wendell and Marilyn fifty dollars a month and the Sewards said, *"Yes."* Marilyn had done some preliminary scouting regarding teaching jobs in the public schools, and she would start teaching within a month of their arrival. Things looked a little more "iffy" for Wendell. However, he soon got a job teaching in Yreka. David, after assisting in the move, took a summer job at Azusa Pacific University where he was enrolled for the fall semester. MeriJean started her junior year, and was one unhappy teenager.

For MeriJean the move to Etna felt like her Waterloo. "I left all my friends and activities for this? I turned sixteen two days after we moved there. The high school in Colton had about one hundred fifty students. I started first grade there and went through my sophomore year. Every friend I had was there. And my idea of California…we're talking Southern California and beaches…we are *not* talking Etna, a little town hidden in the mountains and decades behind. It was a real setback to me that God had sent my parents to Etna. I thought God didn't like me. A loving God would never have let that happen to me.

"There was animosity between my mother and me. While I was growing up, she wanted me to live some austere life and be a homebody, and it just didn't seem to me like she was really interested in what I felt or thought. She was always so busy. My friends thought my parents were super-strict. I wasn't allowed to wear the fashionable clothes they did.

"My father and I got along pretty well. I felt he understood me more, but he was not a disciplinarian. And this upset my mother, causing additional animosity. I was aware I was a problem between my parents. So…in simple terms, when we moved to Etna, that's when God and I went to war! It wasn't long before I got into some serious trouble. I didn't do drugs or alcohol then, but there were other things. I had a boyfriend hotwire my parent's car so we could go on a lark. I had a girlfriend mom didn't like and we'd hang out until real late. In those days it was pretty much all about me. I didn't want to hear my mom's opinions about my friends, who I'll admit were really nothing to be proud of. So if she said something, I would just give her the, 'you don't like anything I do' stuff."

"We knew she was going with a boy that was using drugs, but we didn't know for sure she was using them," Marilyn remembers. "Sometimes she wouldn't come home and we'd get in the car and go looking for her. Those were frantic times. Trying to determine how to cope with that situation used up a lot of our mental energy. Those were the years when I started praying on my way to school. I would drive to school and be crying, praying for God to do whatever He needed to do to bring her around. And then trying to get myself all cleared up so that by the time I got to school my face wasn't all red and my eyes all puffy."

In the fall of 1969 MeriJean enrolled in Azusa Pacific University. When starting the second semester she became sick and returned home for a tonsillectomy. Being home was stressful for her, so she worked out a plan to live with her grandparents in Portland and attend Multnomah School of the Bible.

Her boyfriend at that time was in the army but didn't want to go to Vietnam. So in between Azusa and Multnomah, she picked him up in Central Oregon and drove him to Canada, then quickly drove the twenty hours back to her grandparents' place in the Portland, Oregon, area. She gives her take on all this.

"I went to Multnomah School of the Bible, but honestly I was anything but Multnomah material at that point. It was the only way I figured I could get away from home. I couldn't stand staying with the folks because I was still in the rebellious state against the religious rules thing, and in that state of mind I certainly didn't want to discuss anything with my mom.

"I remember her mentioning how, in her early teen years, she had a problem with her dad's legalism, and how sometimes she'd sass her parents when she didn't think they were being fair. And so it was a natural warfare to go against what I considered at that time a legalistic spirit. (I don't think I wanted to understand my mom at that point.) Dad saw it all more for what it really was, that I was just out to get a reaction from people, but it really bugged my mother—and that was fine with me. Dad thought she shouldn't take me so seriously. He was probably right." MeriJean's rebellion overrode her conscience.

Marilyn was constantly doing good stuff with a determination to get things done. She may have been caught off guard when troubles arose, and her response less than what it could or should have been. A common malady is to be so focused and intent on getting things done that we take vital relationships for granted. Compounding the problem is the fact that adults are most always living in a different social framework than their children. Nowadays kids' peers have different habits, mindsets, desires, and other frames of reference, than older generations. A deep desire to understand the younger generations is needed...and this takes time and a caring heart.

Reflection

Sometimes parents make single-ended decisions on pivotal issues without discussing them with their kids, and resentment (with its inherent perils) is spawned. When communication is limited, felt needs can go unexpressed and, therefore, are most often undetected by parents. Parents can't always honor the wishes and desires of their kids, but they can take the time to hear the kids' side of things and give them some reasons for their (the parents') decisions. The time this takes is time well spent. *Time...yes, that is what it takes...time!*

"We hit the ground running," Marilyn shared. "Our first meeting was in the front yard of one of the inviting couples. The next week we rented the Odd Fellows (IOOF) Hall, but the bat-dropping smells (really!) drove us to look for something better. In God's perfect timing the Congregational church became available. It was amazing. Their pastor had just moved, leaving a small group of people, all over sixty-five. They rented the church to us for fifteen dollars a month. It was such a lovely old building. Most of the Congregational folks felt right at home and it was a harmonious relationship. Scott Valley Berean Church was born.

"We had barely settled in our lovely rented home," Marilyn continued, "when it was sold, and we hastily had to move again the week before school started, to a huge, old and very dirty house. We papered, painted, and laid tile madly, believe me!" Still living in that house now more than 40 years later, Marilyn reflects, "Now, looking back, we see God's hand in that 11th-hour move! This house is just a block from the church, and right away we had two Sunday school classes meeting here. It has three stories and three large bedrooms, plus another room on the third floor that can now be used as a makeshift bedroom, and I hope to have a bath upstairs one day. Downstairs there is a living-dining room, kitchen, study, bedroom, bath, and utility room. It is sunny and bright and homey, and it is ideally located. It sits on a triangle block all by itself in the middle of town. We have people over every Sunday afternoon for lunch, and many people drop in during the week. We became so thankful to be so centrally located.

"Right off, Wendell had a fruitful ministry, since these older folk, mostly women, needed someone to care for them. We soon discovered these California folk weren't quite as 'flaky' as we first imagined. All said, they were delighted the Word was again being taught, and the historic old building and its nostalgic atmosphere gave hints of earlier visions and commitments. The transition was smooth and we praised God for His guidance and provision."

Their involvement in the community also began immediately. Marilyn was teaching in a one-room schoolhouse in nearby Quartz Valley, an easy ten-mile drive one way. During that time, Marilyn said, "I love my little one-room school that hosts K thru 8. In some ways it reminds me of my first job in Cedar Creek, Nebraska. It is a dream come true.'"

Wendell was teaching in Yreka at Jackson Street Middle School, which was his preferred age range. This meant a daily twenty-six-mile drive each way over the mountain, but he enjoyed the beauty that came with it. He did have to chain-up a few times some winters, but in twenty-seven years he never missed a day of school because of snow and ice.

"I was invited to start a fifteen-minute radio broadcast once every two weeks," Wendell shared, "and that proved a real benefit in becoming known in the community. I also joined the Chamber of Commerce and the Rotary. We've tried to take part in as much community life as possible, remembering that our mission is to the world, and not just a tiny group of Christians. Jesus wants each and every person touched with His love, and that means we need to take Him to them.

"Once a month, about twenty men from many occupations have been meeting for breakfast at Larry's Tavern, and these meetings have been a real opening for witnessing. The Clipper Club, a purely social couples club, has given us entrance to an entirely different group in the valley. We continually see God's direction in this work, and are truly grateful to be a part of it. Our prayer for the people of this church and all the churches is that the Valley might see us and remark as they did of the disciples, 'Behold, how they love one another.'"

By the time December rolled around, Marilyn wrote in their newsletter, "Each new day seems to bring added assurance that it is God who works in us both to will and to do what He desires. Wendell's Tuesday night Bible class has been a tremendous blessing, all non-Christians or new Christians. And finally we have some Christian young people, many surrendering their lives and inviting Jesus to be their Lord in recent weeks. We have had three baptismal services in a River Jordan setting at one of the ranches, plus a number in other assorted places. The new believers are all now fellowshipping and receiving teaching in various group settings, mainly in homes.

"We have found our teaching and Wendell's radio program to be wonderful contact points for the outlying areas. His warmth, lack of formalness, and sense of humor seem to set people at ease. He makes friends so readily. God graciously provides strength and health; neither one of us has missed a day of work."

Wendell remembered, "When we arrived in Etna we came up with the motto: *'People Not Programs, Relationships Not Religion, Involvement Not Pronouncements.'* We had this printed on some pens to give away, and worked hard to keep it a reality, not just so many noble-sounding words. We wanted to reach all segments of the valley's cultures, but especially the loggers, ranchers, and Native Americans. It wasn't that others would be neglected, but experience has shown us people who had to work when the work was available often didn't find time to go to a church. However, their souls were just as precious to the

Lord as those who were able to attend, and we wanted them to know some people realize that."

This provides insight into why they and this particular church were so effective in impacting a wide variety of society over many years.

Wendell and the church leadership were very sensitive to the community regarding when they would have meetings. "We tried hard not to conflict with popular activities, such as the rodeos held twice a year. On 'Rodeo Sunday' our service was early and short. When the first horse in the parade came into view through the front door, I would stop whatever was going on and tell the folks, 'The parade has started. Let's get out there and watch it.'"

He also dreaded that the church or Christians would seem "religious or judgmental." When someone would condemn another, Wendell would cringe. "How can we expect to reach people if we're criticizing and condemning them? Jesus told us to love one another, even our enemies. If He's living His life in us, then that is what we will be doing -- not just loving Christians, but everyone." All in all, the Sewards garnered the respect of the entire community.

Wendell found fulfillment and joy in teaching "problem" kids at Jackson Street Middle School in Yreka. He looked past their disabilities and problems and focused on each student as having valuable potential, and he considered it his job to help the potential become reality. This took wisdom and skill (not to mention some unorthodox behavior) to not only gain respect but also to bond with the students ...

A fellow mentioned one hot afternoon that he saw Wendell leading his junior high class up the sidewalk back toward school and everyone was eating ice cream. On another occasion, Wendell spanked the wrong kid and then let the kid use the paddle on him. Wendell says, "Of course, all the kids wanted to participate in that!" One of the over-arching benefits of teaching, for Wendell, was seeing the number of kids who went on to successful lives and careers.

Over the years Wendell performed weddings for many of his previous students, and some of their siblings. He became acquainted with many of the families in the region. Word got around and some months he would have one or more weddings a week. Over a forty-year span he averaged nearly two per month.

+ + +

When reading their newsletters covering the next four years, it confounds the senses. The contacts they made; involvements in the local society; opening their home as a haven for healing and hospitality; maintaining super-human schedules. This pace would exhaust most people.

Marilyn elaborated, "Wendell has three separate plays this week. He has three classes of elective Language Arts (8th grade) and he writes his own course of study—drama, speech, journalism, etc. I have thirty-four kids this year (K-8), and I am having a real struggle to stay ahead of the game. We've had many good speakers this year ministering in the church and community; for example, Nicky Cruz, a former gang leader from New York, and Lambert Dolphin, an incredible research physicist from Stanford Research Institute. As the result of Dolphin's visit, two young men came to live with us while trying to get their lives straightened out.

"Wendell is now on the Etna City Council and I've been asked to be president of the N.W. Siskiyou County Teacher's Association. In July we took forty from our congregation (twenty-four kids) to the Overseas Crusades Family Conference at Mount Hermon near Scotts Valley."

She wraps up with, "This whole year has added such a dimension to our lives. We have to count it one of the best of our lives, in joy and satisfaction and increased knowledge of the grace of God. Any discouragements—and of course there have been some—certainly dim in the light of what we have seen God do. As we think ahead about plans—conference grounds, trail camps for problem kids, a local retirement home, opening our own home to more kids—it is so exciting I can hardly wait to live next year!"

Reflection

In the Seward's first three years in Etna, they established a presence and a foundation that God would use in a very significant way in the years to come. All would not be a bed of roses of course, but God knows the formula for using hardships and sufferings as well as successes and joys to accomplish His purposes. The Sewards had a set of priorities that sacrificed their own comfort and resources of time and finances to help meet the needs of others. That they have developed the *habit* of doing this makes them remarkable.

Chapter Seven

Cameos of Love and Grace

"Ideals are God's pictures of Himself,
painted by Himself, hung in the gallery of our souls."
The Pre-eminence of Jesus Christ,
W.A. Crouch

God builds character and hope in and through suffering, not by its absence. The Sewards did not lose their vision or their burden for missions when they were rejected by a missions organization. In time, they would have opportunity to minister in "Jerusalem, Judea, Samaria, and the uttermost parts of the world," (Acts 1:8) but now was the season to bloom where they were planted. They did, and the fragrance was wafted far and wide.

Marilyn directed "The Joyful Noise," a twenty-five-voice youth choir. She took the group to Los Angeles at Christmas-time in 1971. "We sang first at upscale Mariner's church, then in a Black church in the Watts area pastored by Ralph Houston, who is also owner of the A&A Barrel Co. in Los Angeles. We all stayed with the families there, and had such a warm, loving time together. Out of that grew a return visit from the Black church to Scott Valley in July of the next year. Forty-eight of these inner-city folk spent a week with us in our homes when not camping in the mountains. The climax of their visit was a Sunday morning concert. Their youth choir sounded like a tremendous pipe organ and sang with ours. The love was so tangible and real it seemed like a foretaste of heaven. A joint baptismal service at the river Sunday afternoon ended a most moving, precious week; one of the highlights of our lives, I'm sure."

Marilyn continues in a newsletter from that period, "One of our joys has been the succession of kids God has brought to our home, including two fellows, Brian and Ron, who Lambert Dolphin sent three years ago. I had been praying for some Christian young men for the young women in our church, but I was a little startled when Brian and Ron knocked on our door, looking so much like 'flower children' from Haight-Ashbury. They were fresh out of the pot-LSD drug culture, new Christians, stopping for a brief visit…which lasted for years. We had a houseful of kids at the time, and there were often eight or ten of us at the dinner table. Ron and Brian were not exactly into the Christian culture, and more than once, were denied entrance to a restaurant because of no shoes or no shirt. But they grew in grace and we loved them a lot. Overhearing me wish for a bay window in my kitchen, they tore out the wall one day while we were at school, and with the help of our carpenter friends from the neighborhood, built my bay window…and went on to build bedrooms on the third floor and a new garage.

"At this point, Brian has been at Biola (Bible Institute of Los Angeles) for almost two years now, and is doing so well. Ron is still with us, a real student of the Word, an excellent carpenter, and the stable element in our home, as some of the others come and go. These include Becky, Tim, Mike, Don, Jim, Rick, Dean, Paul, and presently Gus, twenty-one." When Brian finished at Biola he returned to Etna to become the Assistant Pastor for a time. He and Ron became licensed contractors later on.

"Gus came to us as a new Christian, still struggling with alcohol and drug addictions. He so badly wanted to be God's person, but the addiction had a grip on him that kept us on high alert. We'd find six-packs under his bed, and more than once, Wendell spent midnight hours scouring the country for Gus and one of our exchange students who had taken an unlicensed pickup without permission, of course, and had gone off on a joy ride. Eventually Gus had to leave because he was stealing money from local merchants to buy liquor. Years later he called to apologize for his behavior. He had finally gotten the counseling he needed and was free and clean. He became a pastor and took in young people like himself. He told us it was mainly Wendell's influence that led him in this path.

"Juhani, our eighteen-year-old exchange student from Finland, is a talented pianist, a ham radio operator and a Christian. Paul, who had been with us for a year, was married three weeks ago to Debbie, one of our girls, in one of the loveliest weddings ever during the Sunday evening service. There was no big fuss but a lot of sweetness and love spilled over. Wendell did such a good job with the service. He always makes it a delightful and meaningful time."

The Sewards at this time (end of 1972) had been in Etna five years, and it was amazing what had transpired during that time. They had become well established in the community in their public school teaching roles. The church, with about two hundred attending, was growing with a steady stream of new believers. Marilyn's report above provides insights into one of the ways they worked out their vision and heart for missions. Their hospitality and evident loving care made their home a haven of comfort and healing. Dozens found their way to the Sewards' doors…those always open doors. Each person entering was made to feel loved and valuable.

A significant occurrence in 1973 shook the whole valley. A group of young adults, none of them churchgoers or professed Christians, hung out together. Eight of the girls were known as the Can-Can Girls. They were attractive but a little rough around the edges. Dressed in their Can-Can outfits they performed at a variety of festivities. A friend of one of the girls in the group, Bill Johnson, a very popular boy from a pioneering family and known throughout the valley, contracted leukemia and the prognosis was not good. As Bill's condition worsened, his fiancée Francyne, a baby Christian, and a friend of hers prayed with Bill to receive Christ. He died shortly afterward. Francyne, having visited the Berean church to ask for prayer for Bill had met Wendell. She asked him if he would do the funeral, and of course Wendell readily agreed.

Bill's death sent a shockwave through their group. Many in the valley were awakened to the realities of life and death, setting some extraordinary things into motion. Marilyn, writing at the end of 1973, mentioned, "This fall God used the death of a popular young man, Bill Johnson, a new believer, to bring a whole circle of his family and friends to Himself, and that circle is still widening."

Hit hard, the group of friends who lived life somewhat frivolously, without much thought of spiritual things, suddenly became aware of their need to make their lives right with God. In a short time they all became close to the Sewards, especially five of the Can-Can Girls, spending a lot of time in the Sewards' home. Wendell, and later Marilyn, would also meet these girls and a few others in one of their homes in Callahan, a small town twelve miles south of Etna. They discussed

God and what it meant to know Him, and one by one these five Can-Can Girls came to make Jesus their Lord, as did several of their friends. Francyne, the sister to one of the Can-Can Girls, said in reflection, "I practically lived at the Sewards' for a few months. Recently I was in their home and they still have the same couch almost thirty years later. Wow…I wonder how many lives have been changed while sitting on that couch?" A bunch!

We learn a few more details from Diane, another member of the Can-Can group. We also get a glimpse of Wendell's gifts and humor. Diane tells, "Wendell just totally accepted us the way we were. We all smoked and drank when we were Can-Canning. Wendell didn't care. He loved us. He started coming to one of our houses to visit just to see how everybody was doing. That's how Wendell is. He decided that it would be nice if we could get together once a week for lunch. So we'd meet at somebody's house and have lunch and he would meet us there.

"Before long he started sharing from the Bible, and then we started having Bible studies. So bless his heart, every time he would come he insisted we keep smoking so we'd be comfortable. Poor guy, it must have just about killed him, all that smoke.

"His warm and sincere ways were leading us to the Lord. He met with us for several months. Then Marilyn decided we needed a little more solid food. Kind of like, 'Okay, Wendell—you stay home. I'll go meet with the girls.' So she did and we had some very intense Bible studies with her. Through them we all became Christians. Wendell baptized me in the Scott River while Marilyn read a scripture. Once at rodeo time, Wendell wanted us girls to come to church dressed in our costumes. We did and that created a major stir. But Wendell thought it was great. You always felt loved and accepted by Wendell. He knows more about showing Jesus than anyone I've ever known."

Bill's best friend, Jerry, shares, "After Bill's death I was distraught. I had bad dreams and a lot of emotional pain. Wendell did the funeral and that was only the second or third time I had ever been in a Protestant church. I met Wendell afterward and he said he'd like to meet me again. After that I reached out to Wendell and we began spending a lot of time together, and I gave my life to Christ. Right after that, Wendell baptized me in Etna Creek…man, that was cold…and Ed Murphy, a missionary with Overseas Crusades, who was in town speaking, read the scripture."

Judy, another of the Can-Can Girls, many years later lost her own battle with cancer. Just before her exodus this oh-so-precious saint shared with Judi and me, "Wendell was just so wonderful. I mean I can't even say... (choked up). When we first started going to church we saw other people we knew and we said to him, 'We feel like a lot of people here are like Sunday morning Christians.' And he said, 'You need to be looking up, not around.' I've tried to always remember that. They let us grow at our own speed and they made no judgments whatsoever. Our concept of Christianity was that we had to give up everything we were doing which we thought was fun at the time, and lead this straight and narrow life, and I'm sure a lot of people think that way.

"But Wendell wouldn't condemn us no matter what. Pretty soon most of us got married, and our entertainment was going to Corrigan's Bar on Saturday night. We girls wondered, 'What are we going to do? We can't do that, now that we're going to church.'

"And Wendell said, 'Hey, the worst thing you could do is stop because then your husbands are going to get upset with you. You can go—you don't have to drink. When God convicts you that you need to stop doing those things, then it's time to quit. Not when people around you are saying you should quit.'

"Well, that surprised us, so we continued for a while and then our husbands began accepting Christ too so pretty soon we all quit going there. These days I find it is the religious people who get upset with Wendell, not the others. It isn't church doctrines that define Wendell and Marilyn's lives, it's their love and acceptance."

Reflection

Think for a minute...why did the people seek out Jesus? Because He loved them, understood them, and ministered to them in several different ways to meet their felt and real needs. He didn't condemn or criticize them, but had compassion on them. We see this same phenomena with the Sewards. Giving up our rights to ourselves; living outside any protective shell; seeing value in every person and helping others find meaning in life is doing it right. Showing love, acceptance and forgiveness is always right no matter the context.

✝ ✝ ✝

While 1973 was winding down, Marilyn sat at the dining room table pecking away at the typewriter. "I'm taking my school kids to see the Nutcracker Ballet in Ashland this Wednesday night; the Joyful Noise is almost ready for our Christmas program this Thursday night. Wendell's school is having their share of programs and he's involved in some of that. Our household has changed almost completely this year. Ron, with us for almost three years, moved home in April. Juhani flew home to Finland in July, only to be replaced by Robert Dagys from Uruguay, in August. Dean and Kelly (our only girl), both seniors, and Ronnie, a sophomore, complete our quartet of high-schoolers. Others have come and gone during the year, some here for the summer, others for only a few months—Bill, Dwight, Glenn, Greg, Jim, Gus, Pam, Susie, Kathy and her little Danielle (more on these two later)…the length of the list even surprises me! Some of these kids have had real problems.

"Wendell and I would often spend hours listening and talking with the kids trying to really learn their hearts, and to give them a sense of hope and direction for their lives. The kids that had messed up their lives on drugs or alcohol were real challenges. Most really wanted to get their lives straightened out, but their habit had reached the disease stage, and this isn't easy to overcome. Understanding the situation they were in when they began their abuse often provided information we needed to help them overcome it. Our basic premise was that each kid was valuable and had great potential. And it was our responsibility to love and try to understand them, not to criticize or condemn them. For them the key to victory was hope and belief—believing they could be overcomers.

"If anyone would have told us six years ago that we'd find six-packs of beer under the beds, or marijuana accidentally (you'd better believe accidentally!) dropped on the bathroom floor, we'd have laughed in disbelief. Nobody's laughing now! Sometimes we say, 'Thanks a lot, Lord. I've learned all the patience I need now, so how about changing the program?' Last spring we were ready for a vacation from kids, but God seemed to have other plans with all the guests we had. He always does provide a way through the problems of the moment—never around them, or away from them, but through them. Oh, how grateful we are to be included in His plans.

"We've realized more than ever that the reality of the Christian life involves a tremendous amount of risk-taking, making ourselves completely open and vulnerable, with an absolute trust in God, and recognition of the *resurrection power* that is ours. It certainly puts a different glow on the Christian life.

"I don't ever want this annual *share time* to sound like we just go from one great victory to another out here. Honestly, when I begin to recap the year, all the hard times, frustration, despair, and loneliness which beset us seem to dim into inconsequence and I end up having my own private Thanksgiving as I recall what God has performed. I don't know what this adds to your holiday, but it surely enhances ours! This has been another in a series of exciting, strenuous years. Sometimes we feel like rubber bands, stretched in all directions. The facets of our lives have multiplied this year, and I surely do remind the Lord of a verse given to us on our wedding day: *'As thy days, so shall thy strength be.'*"[1]

> *"The color and sparkle (even tears sparkle) of our days, the surprise elements of our lives are lavishly splashed on by a big God who delights in giving His children "abundantly above what they could ask or expect." Thank you, God, for the "wonder of it all." It's obvious that PEOPLE are the brushes you use to paint life's portrait—what a varied supply you have" (Marilyn Seward)*

---

1   Deuteronomy 33:25

Chapter Eight

Showcase Relationships

*"When our eyes see our hands doing the work of our hearts…
the doors of our souls fly open and love steps forth to heal everything
in sight."*
Michael Bridge

In the mountains and valleys of Northern California, the snow, without any fanfare, can reach significant depth in a relatively short period of time. Quietly descending, the size of large corn-flakes, the soft pristine blanket by mid-afternoon was over a foot deep, smoothing the landscape without blemish or wrinkle. The exceptions were the indentations in the snow left by friends departing to their cars after lunch.

The dishes were washed and stashed, the kitchen and dining room swept; it was late afternoon and time for a rest. Marilyn settled into the stuffed chair with a sigh, closed her eyes hoping for a short nap when a gentle knock came at the door. "I wonder who that is?" she mumbled to Wendell, whose head was sandwiched in the Sacramento Bee. A grunt could be heard above the headline, "Marijuana: Northern California's New Cash Crop?" Marilyn opened the door.

"Hi. My name is Kathy and I'm from the Marbles. The pass is snowed in and I don't have chains. Someone told me to come see you about spending the night."

"Oh, you dear things. Come in out of the snow. How old is the baby?"

"She's eighteen months."

"My heavens, those clothes look awfully wet. Aren't you freezing? We need to get you into some dry clothes while I dry those. Sure, you can spend the night here. I'll bet you're hungry too."

"A little…yes."

"When did you come over the mountain? Are you over here for something special?"

"I came over this morning to go to church. I heard this church was special from someone who visited our mining claim and I wanted to visit."

"Well, let's get those clothes changed and some warm soup into you; then we can have a chat. Do you have any dry clothes in the car?"

"No…I didn't think we'd be staying over."

"Well, that's no problem. Come with me and we'll find something for you both while these are drying. This is my husband Wendell…"

"Hi!"

"Dear, would you go check on the quilts and stuff in the upper room?"

To Kathy: "We have a nice little bedroom up on the third floor with a baby-bed. There are people in the two bedrooms on the second floor, but you won't bother them. You can use our bathroom down here through our bedroom right there if the one up there is busy."

"Thank you." A tear was making its way down a cheek reddened from the cold.

Pulling the baby's clothes from the dryer, Marilyn could see they (and Kathy's) were meager and worn. Living in a tent in the rugged Marble Wilderness Area with a group prospecting for gold, many miles of rocky trails from any store, was tough on any account. With a small child it was stressful and exhausting. Money was scarce until the "strike" came …and in Kathy's case this hadn't yet occurred.

After graduating from prestigious Cubberly High School in Palo Alto, California, Kathy spent one year in college and then ran off with her boy friend, heading for a commune in Dunsmuir, California, a small railroad town tucked away in a valley near the base of imposing fourteen-thousand-foot Mount Shasta. It was the summer of 1969. A year later, the couple, with some friends, drifted into the nearby Marble Mountains where they staked out several mining claims. They had been working these mines the past two-plus years. Life was tough and food sparse; loving companionship and marijuana—plentiful.

After Kathy became pregnant, she had felt a need to grow closer to God, and began reading the New Testament given her as a birthday gift years earlier. She had been carrying it as a good luck charm. Eventually, and with two other girls living in tents in the same general area of the mountains, she began regularly reading and re-reading the New Testament with them. The words did often seem to have life, and she felt God really understood her heart. She developed a real hunger for the words, never seeming to get enough.

"When I read of Jesus' love for all of us in the world, and how he expressed that love by giving his life so we could live, I felt I had discovered a meaning and purpose for my life. I wanted to know more and to do more. When a friend of one of the girls who came to visit told us about this real warm and friendly church in Etna, I knew someday I wanted to go there." She tucked this knowledge away in her memory..

Winters are unpredictable in the northern mountains. Early and late snows are quite commonplace, often moving in without warning. Some are notably providential. Kathy never returned to the mountains. She and her child lived with the Sewards a little over a year.

Wendell called Kathy his "recycled Hippie," and referred to her that way ever after. She and little Danielle lived in the Sewards' home at the same time as Ron, Juhani, and other occasional residents.

Kathy is now dean of the math department of a community college near Sacramento, California. The Sewards helped her find work, daycare for her daughter, and assisted in her entering college. Later, when she married Joe McClain, Wendell performed the ceremony. The couple had another daughter. Both daughters are successful businesswomen.

Kathy describes it this way: "While I was living with the Sewards it wasn't the Sewards' expectation that I had to do something or become something. They just accepted me for me. Marilyn was so insightful and loving, and although we had some awkward times early on, I learned to respect her highly…and Wendell too. They were willing to talk at any time, and were understanding. I was amazed at how they understood people. I think it's because they loved everybody. Wendell was so easy to be around, always loving and sympathetic…and if I had a tough question, he would tell me what he thought…then he would ask Marilyn what she thought. Her wisdom always surprised me. I'd ask myself, 'How does she know these things?' The two of them…they saved my life."

Marilyn recalls, "When Kathy and Danielle first came, we had to make some adjustments in our thinking and our behavior. They were both dirty and undisciplined, and in rags more or less. I can still see little Danielle sitting in her high chair just throwing food everywhere.

She was used to living in the outdoors or in a tent, and certainly wasn't 'house-broken.' Kathy and I had some tough moments from time to time. She would get on my case: *'You don't have to teach me how to raise my child.'*

"What I remember more vividly are the great discussions we had. Kathy was a sharp girl, and I soon learned she was a responsible person who was willing to do what it took to live responsibly. It was that initiative that brought her to us. We used to sit and share about life and philosophize, and I gained a real love and appreciation for her, who, although she had taken the 'adventurous' route early in life to pursue freedom and satisfy fleshly desires, now wanted to make something of herself and her daughter. Although gradual, you could definitely see the change in their behavior. Wendell and I had a strong feeling she was going to be okay… and she is. She's such a sweetheart…she and her whole family."

Seemingly trapped by a surprisingly early snow, God turned their dilemma into a liberating experience, using the Sewards' love and care—to generate security and hope.

Reflection

Acceptance and trust is conducive to the positive development of a person's true personality. When people sense we 'expect' a certain level of behavior, it is an intimidation, and often not a good one. People might recede into a shell, or seeds of resentment and/or resistance can germinate. Building a mutually trustful friendship requires accepting people where they are, and then allowing love and understanding to guide the way. This is one of the Sewards' greatest strengths.

Early in 1974, Wendell and Marilyn attended a pastors' conference at Mount Hermon Conference Center, a place that was to become quite familiar to them. Part of what attracted them was a young man speaking on *"Why I Don't Go To Church."*

Marilyn remembers the meeting: "We were most drawn to a young couple, the Mike Yaconellis, from San Diego. He published the *Wittenberg Door*, a unique Christian magazine. He shared his frustrations with the legalistic Church, and we felt definitely led to invite him and his wife to visit Scott Valley. (What Marilyn doesn't say here was they bought a plane ticket and sent it down to Mike with the invitation. Mike was shocked—but went; he felt some strange attraction to this couple.) They came—twice—and, to our surprise and theirs, were unanimously called to start a new church in Yreka."

Mike co-owned Youth Specialties, an organization specializing in equipping youth workers for reaching out in culturally relevant methods to kids from all segments of contemporary society with God's truth and love. He traveled widely, including abroad. He had a lot on his platter, including some personal issues causing him turmoil.

He and Wendell began spending a lot of time together, and Wendell often would do the teaching for Mike when Mike was traveling. Marilyn said, "Now we are excited. We don't know what God has in mind, but that's the neat thing about this Christian life—the absolute assurance He has it all in mind, and it's not something that takes Him by surprise."

Mike shared with me on one occasion how, once he understood Wendell's motives and lifestyle, he felt totally comfortable with him and often sought his counsel. He said, "I found Wendell quick to listen, and he accepted me no matter what. I was going through some deep struggles on a couple of fronts, and he always had a listening ear and never condemned me, always accepting me as I was. My turmoils needed the wisdom and calming effect of his warm heart and understanding. As I spent more time with him I saw he was living the life of love and grace I had been expounding on and getting into trouble for." (Wendell got into trouble for it also, according to some sources.)

Later, Mike said, when he was going through divorce, it seemed the Sewards were a little distant. "At that point I was wondering how to leave the planet." Marilyn had really been hard on Mike for his seeming lack of commitment in the marriage. "Then," she relates, "one day God said to me, 'Marilyn, you have a judgmental spirit toward Mike Yaconelli and that is wrong.' I was so convicted. I called him and asked him to come for dinner, and I sat right here and had to ask his forgiveness. I was so wrong. From that point on our relationship took on new life, and when Mike married his new wife, Karla, Wendell and I were totally supportive."

Over the years Mike invited them to attend the annual National Youth Workers Conventions that Youth Specialties hosted. The Sewards enjoyed watching the thousands of youth ministers listen to speakers and being set free from legalistic and paralyzing church traditions.

It is remarkable how some seeming little incident can turn into a life-changing phenomenon. This was often the case with Wendell and Marilyn. They would attend many conferences and seminars only to find someone there who they thought should come share in Scott Valley. Many speakers were invited and came, resulting in new understandings of God's Grace at work in the world.

In 1979, Mike Yaconelli and Wendell attended the National Prayer Breakfast in Washington, D.C., and spent time with their mutual friend, Senator Mark Hatfield from Oregon. From my view, these were three peas in the same pod. All had experienced a *break-through* into the life-giving, refreshing waters of unconditional love and acceptance. These living waters produced in them a desire for servant-hood, humility, grace, acceptance, and freedom—and a *break-away* from legalism, put-downs, and prejudice. It seems so hard for the Church to get an experiential understanding of the profoundly simple truth of "...love, faith and hope remain...and the greatest of these is love."[1]

"Visiting talent blesses the community and the church." Marilyn is writing in a 1976 newsletter. "Brennan Manning, a Catholic author and inspiring speaker who leads spiritual retreats and has a ministry with the poor, came for a weekend. Manning is refreshing and challenging, helping people who have only known traditional religion move into a deeper relationship with Jesus and with one another. Another program led by singer Johnny Ray Watson was held at the high school along with a BBQ and pie auction. It was very well attended by a wide spectrum of folks in the Valley, and several responded to his low-key invitation to consider the claims of Christ.

"God did exceedingly above when Joyce Landorf was here in November for our Fall Banquet (two hundred fifty guests). Joyce was just right for Scott Valley, and we are still hearing of families changed by her ministry—so much impact that we've just arranged for her and

---

1   1 Corinthians 13:13

Dr. James Dobson (*Dare to Discipline*) to be here for a Family Forum September 9-11, 1976."

Following this up in December of '76, Marilyn wrote, "Our Family Forum in September with Joyce Landorf and Dr. James Dobson in Yreka and Scott Valley brought out over three hundred thirty people, and was all we hoped it to be in changing family lives. The Sunday morning Berean-Methodist service with Joyce at the high school was a demonstration of the spirit of unity that is developing here in the Valley. Joyce's message on acceptance was one we all needed to hear and put into our lives"

Luis Palau held a crusade in nearby Grants Pass, Oregon, in September.[2] Marilyn remembers, "We took many a carload up night after night, and many people had life-changing experiences. We had met Luis earlier at the OC Family Conference at Mount Hermon."

Mr. Palau, in his book, *The Schemer and the Dreamer,* indicates that he had already been impressed by the Sewards when he wrote, "We know a couple in a little town called Etna in Northern California. There are only five hundred fifty people in Etna, but the Lord has used this couple to reach out to hundreds of people all over the western United States. We have heard testimonies of teens who had been on drugs, whom God has delivered through their ministry… To me their lives have always been a tremendous example of how God can use lives totally given to Him... Something is happening in Etna that is powerful, for the glory of God."

Reflection

It is remarkable how a seemingly small incident or act of kindness can evolve into a life-changing phenomenon. All significant things have a beginning somewhere, somehow. A knock on the door, a statement a speaker makes, or something you read in a book can initiate an unexpected experience and unforeseeable outcome. When the equation contains a willingness to be involved, genuine concern and love, and unselfishness with resources, there is a high likelihood that everyone concerned will be a winner.

---

2   My wife, Judi, and I helped coordinate this "first in the US" Palau crusade, being on the Luis Palau Evangelistic Team at the time, which then was an arm of Overseas Crusades (now OCI).

Chapter Nine

Four Transformations

"I began to wonder if becoming a Christian did not work more like falling in love than agreeing with some true principles".
Donald Miller, *Searching For God Knows What*

One thing that has helped the Sewards sort through and understand the difference between what is *wrong* and what is simply *different* is the variety of students (usually sixteen to eighteen years of age) from different cultures and continents who have lived in their home. Eventually the Sewards would host thirty-six foreign students for a school year or longer. Marilyn, being the local representative for Youth For Understanding, also helped place students in other homes and towns. Shortly after the turn of the century while traveling through Europe I would seek out and interview some of these students. The following testimonies come from ex-students who stayed in the Sewards' home between 1972 and 1980.

Harold Kuhn, a Volkswagen employee living in Kassell, Germany, twenty-two years later reflected back to his time in the Sewards' home as we were assembling a crib for his newborn daughter:

"Marilyn has a lot of energy and a lot of sensitivity. She knows how to talk to people; she is insightful and has a very practical mind. She can give good advice and still not be pushy. She gives you the feeling that you have the freedom to do whatever you want. And she knows how to get people together to get something accomplished.

"And Wendell—um, well, first of all, he's really a gifted speaker. He has a lot of humor and a different way of reaching out to people than Marilyn. He reaches them with his humor and melts down the barriers with his casual way. He seemed to stress that love is the thing, and he… how do you say that… the truths he communicates are the things he lives out?"

Harold also observed, "There was often someone coming in and staying for days and sometimes weeks, and definitely there were always visitors on the weekend. After church we would have a big meal with many people either in the house or out in the yard. I think everybody considered them to be an extraordinary couple because of the way they related to people and were always bringing them together. They are a very special couple, ready to help anyone. When I returned to Germany and went to church here, there was not that same love and friendship. I began to miss the Sewards, but my wife and I finally found some other Christians we meet with in our homes. I try to accept others unconditionally like the Sewards accepted me."

Marilyn recalls, "When Harold was living with us, he had problems with depression and fear. I remember sitting up with him one night until 2 a.m., trying to soothe him. He had gone to a war movie and it really got to him and he couldn't sleep and was plagued with fear and depression. I also remember, he and another fellow living with us kept picking on a Japanese boy also living here who was quiet; but one day he blew up and attacked both the guys. Things were really quiet for a long time after that. Just recently, though, Harold told me he visited Fuiigi when he was in Japan for Volkswagen. This is nearly thirty years later."

Uwe (oo-vay) Brietkopf is a photo-journalist living in Wiesbaden. Uwe started off our interview with, "I didn't know where I was going when I got to America. Someone gave me a ticket to Medford, Oregon, and told me someone would pick me up. My thoughts were that nobody wanted to have me. Later I found my concerns were so wrong because it was one of the greatest experiences of my life to stay there that year. It opened up many dimensions of life and new horizons I wouldn't have realized otherwise."

I asked Uwe if he felt encouraged by the Sewards. He replied, "Oh, yes—definitely, and I had so much respect for the Sewards because they never pushed me to believe in God or to become a Christian. They showed me their lives and their beliefs. It's a German thing to have your head straightened out very early in life—know what you are going to do and how to study and how to make your life happen.

But the main thing I took back from the year in their home is there is so much more. Your basic life, the real you, has to come from within yourself, not from the outside. They showed me God living in them and I wanted Him to live in me like that. I still do.

"I could hardly believe how Marilyn could organize her life so she could do so many things with such flair and efficiency. She would come home from school and maybe a meeting with a big bag of food. Ten minutes later the food was on the table. She's very intelligent and very efficient at the same time. Successful people are often thought to have little emotion. What impressed me with Marilyn was if you had an emotional problem she would talk to you and had the amazing gift to understand it. And she had a very tender heart, and would cry with those who were crying. She knew how to deal with emotional problems and psychological problems and spiritual problems at the same time, and have feeling in doing it. This is hard to put in words."

Hmmm…It's harder to put into life!

"When I learned Wendell was a reverend, I felt a little nervous. How do you act in the home of a reverend? But he was so down-to-earth and has a good sense of humor and so I soon felt relaxed. He was interested in my sports. I broke two school records in track and field. I'm a runner. When school was out, they said we were going to celebrate by going to Hawaii, Wendell's treat. I just couldn't believe it. We went for two weeks! More than I could dream!"

After we returned, he took me on an episode…is that what you say? We went up into the mountains to a logging camp where he performed a wedding. That was special. The forest seemed like such a special place for that. I'll never forget it."

Uwe then said something very profound. "That gave me a whole new picture of Christianity, you know. It is life; wherever you go, it is just life and love! I used to think it was in the cathedrals, but that wasn't for me. But it is just in living day by day, and loving and caring for people wherever you go. With the Sewards I experienced life wherever we went!"

"Natasha was sixteen when she lived with us. She hailed from Wiesbaden, Germany, and was an avid tennis player, becoming a star on the Etna High School tennis team. A definite highlight of her stay here was we were able to take her to Portland to see Boris Becker play. This young man had just won the Wimbledon. Natasha was able to talk to him, really making her day! It is so wonderful when you can be involved in helping someone's dream come true and make them feel special. You want to bless them if you can."

Twenty years later I interviewed Natasha, now a children's dentist, in Wiesbaden. She had gone back to Germany and found the churches cold and dead, so she quit going. She shared her impression of the Sewards.

"I think the best Bible teaching is to watch Wendell and Marilyn. They just live it. They're living it all day long. If somebody is sick, Marilyn is cooking for them, and Wendell is visiting them. Somebody needs a car, no problem—they have an extra one. Marilyn is compassionate but also extremely organized and on the go. Wendell is more laid back. I think if you have a problem, it's easier to talk to Wendell. He really doesn't have to solve everything at the moment. He's very calm and a very good person. If you are a Christian or not a Christian, he sees the good things in you. He can find them."

The Sewards' home was a continual haven for the needy. In addition to foreign students, there were other students from nearby but remote areas, and periodically itinerant and temporary workers who found refuge there. Additionally, there were many who had behavioral problems and serious needs who came from the river valleys, mountains, and towns and cities, looking for help and someone who cared. They came from a broad spectrum of social and economic strata ranging from the well-to-do to the down-and-outers. Many came from parents baffled in how to treat and heal the deep-rooted problems in their teenagers. Some were pregnant, many abused drugs or alcohol, some needed a roof over their heads, and/or a shoulder to cry on. Some were working people needing a place for a short time until they could find something else.

From wherever they came, and for whatever reason, they were almost never turned away, unless the Sewards thought there was a more appropriate place for them, and then they would help them get there.

They were never heavy-handed or demanding and had simple, civil rules of behavior (help with certain chores, keep your space clean, etc.), and those staying there were never pressed regarding their beliefs or behavior.

The Sewards both taught, except in the summertime, and therefore interaction with them was relegated to breakfast and dinner, evenings and weekends. They did not push any expectations on their guests except to be civil to one another; and this was more or less taken for granted. From these and other testimonies we learn that whatever took place, it was effective for transforming lives. Wendell and Marilyn always tried to see everyone through Jesus' eyes and heart. They see positive, intrinsic value in every created person. They don't have to think twice to offer a kind word, a warm meal, or a comfortable bed to whomever comes through their doors in need.

Yolanda, from the nearby Salmon River Valley, shares her amazing story. She came to the Sewards in 1973. First a word about the Salmon River. In these Northern California mountains near the Oregon border, there are remote valleys, many of them hosting rivers. The Salmon River flows to the west into the Klamath River that spills into the Pacific Ocean. It is one of the more remote areas, and in the sixties became a haven for hippies and pot-growers, loggers, and miners. There are remnants to this day. One doesn't ask many questions in "them parts." Some remnants want to be anonymous.

Now, over thirty years later, Yolanda provides some insights into why so many have sought Wendell and Marilyn out. We get an inside-look into the Sewards' lives. Hers is yet another of many similar testimonies:

"I was down on the Salmon River; I was pretty much left on my own. There was a lot of drugs and stuff. I grew up in the thick of it. I don't want to talk about the details. But for some reason, being the oldest of four kids, I felt like I had to take care of everybody. I saw what it was doing to people; I didn't want to have any part of it. I would take our dogs for long walks down the road and think, *I know somebody is watching out for me, and I'm going to be somebody special someday, so I just need to hang on.*" Yolanda's beautiful blue eyes were moist...

"We had contacted several people that were hosting River kids so they could go to high school in Etna seventy miles away, but there was no place for me to stay. A high school friend told me to contact the Sewards because they had people living there. Some were foreign students. So I went to their house. I was fourteen. After questioning me they said, 'that's fine, we'd be glad for you to stay here, and we'd like you to go to Sunday school, which is in our living room, and also to church,' where Wendell was pastoring. This was no problem for me.

"I came from a really rough background and I was probably the worst child you ever met. Wendell and Marilyn didn't pass judgment or anything. I remember the first Sunday I went to church I slept through the entire service. Wendell was speaking. I'd never been to church before except once in San Jose and it scared me to death and it made me think for sure I was going to hell no matter what!

"Wendell never said a word to me about sleeping. I enjoyed meeting the people and the classes in their home. The understanding I got of being a Christian was new to me, because I hadn't realized it was mainly loving and accepting and caring, and that God would actually come into my own life and help me live that way. I really was thankful for so many things and I wanted to please God. It wasn't long before I accepted Christ and from then on I've always been excited about life and want to show people God loves them.

"I feel like Wendell and Marilyn were my saviors. I came from nothing, didn't know anything, and I had nowhere to live. They took me in and gave me the solid foundation of Jesus Christ. Marilyn and I didn't always see eye to eye. I was a rough little girl! I had no manners. So Marilyn and I had some struggles, but they never judged me. I learned a lot about how to live while I was in their home.

"I was surprised they always kept their doors unlocked so people could come in to talk to them anytime. Every Sunday after church we'd have a roast and mashed potatoes and invite a family or two over, or if there were new people they were always invited. If kids came we'd play air hockey or pool upstairs. It was a real home. One Christmas we made a metal star and Wendell went up the ladder outside and we handed it to him out the third story window. It is still there!"

We asked Yolanda how she would characterize each of the Sewards.

"Wendell is very sensitive; he is Marilyn's sensitive side. He is very loving and very caring and you know he is happy to see you. He just wants to sit and talk and take the time, no matter where you are. He has the biggest heart. I don't know how else to describe it. He's soft-spoken and thoughtful and… Marilyn has the hammer."

I laughed.

"No-no-no…not in a bad way; don't get me wrong. They compliment each other perfectly.

"Marilyn's not a touchy-feely person, but she's there; you know when you need her, she's always there. If I called her up and said, 'Hey, I need to talk to you,' she would listen to me very patiently then she'd say, 'Well, this is what you need to do.' And she'd put me on the right track—whether I liked it or not. But she could also be very loving and I've watched her give so many clothes and food and money to people. When she's counseling someone she is very sweet and understanding, yet she has the ability to always get to the heart of the matter and suggest a way to go."

In wrapping up our time together, Yolanda added, "They are the only people I know who have been married for sixty years! All the doors were always wide open in the house, they had nothing to hide. Even when they slept, the door was open. We were welcome to go into their bedroom and sit or sleep on the bed. They didn't ever keep anybody out. And they've never had anything stolen. That is absolutely amazing! They are just there for everybody. That's like Jesus." Yolanda, now an award-winning real estate broker, continues to live in the area.

Marilyn reflects, "We count every person that comes through our doors a new learning experience for us, no matter who they are or where they come from. Each one is an individual with his or her own set of needs, hopes and values, and each one has something special about them that God put there, and we appreciate and learn from these unique personalities. Some are like oysters where the grit and grind of the world has resulted in producing a pearl of grace. Some have lived lives of relative calm. Some are mild and soft-spoken, and others are strong-willed and extroverts. We learn something of value from each of them that we can use in our own lives. Even in the midst of all the hustle-bustle turmoil, we draw strength from their love and affection. God knows what each one of us needs, and He is not through with any of us." Blessed is our destiny!

Reflection

These four 'live-in' reflections are tributaries of living water, flowing from a fountain of loving care and wisdom, spawning their own streams to flow in innumerable and endless journeys, multiplying love and hope.

Blessed is Our Destiny
O God, we cannot fathom eternity with you....yet we know it's true.
Blessed is our destiny!
To look beyond the far beyond past present faith and mind,
And see the untold mysteries held safe for those who find
That such a reality exists.
Who will know? Who can see this life past life?
And see the living God face to face?
How can it be that any would see
Thy perfect glory and majesty?
That dwells in all eternity?
Before time began, you set your joy
So it would grow--as both your love and fullness dwelled
In those who in time beheld - your Son.
Bob Waymire[1]

Chapter Ten

Kidder Creek Orchard Camp

*"Looking back, the spiritual awaking and foundation I received
at camp set the compass for the remainder of my life."*
Reflection of a KCOC alumnus

It was 1976 and Marilyn was explaining, "We are finally getting a Christian camp in the valley. This has been a goal of ours for years. God has sent the Joneses to us from the successful Wolf Mountain Camp they founded near Grass Valley, California, in the foothills of the Sierras. Against great odds they, with the help of some churches and individuals, were able to make a securing payment on a lovely three hundred thirty-three acre ranch tucked in a little valley of its own only six miles from Etna. It has three hundred twenty apple trees, a saw mill, a home, barns, farm equipment, plus mountains, springs, and breath-taking scenery. It is located on a year-around stream, Kidder Creek; hence, it was named Kidder Creek Orchard Camp. Since Wendell and I met at Maranatha Camp way back in 1943, we've been very camp-conscious, and also excited to see this dream become a reality. In the future we see, God willing, a horse camp, back-packing, swimming, and other activities."

Camp founders, Dick and Norma Jones, are retired now and live on property adjacent to the camp. Dick was eighty when he told us:

"When the camp started, Wendell and Marilyn spearheaded everything. They are the ones that carried it, really. They had the vision, they understood the outreach of it, and they had the experience and the gifts. They met at a Christian camp you know. Initially some thought, 'Well, the Sewards will want the camp to come under the Berean umbrella,' but Wendell and Marilyn were against that. They didn't think it should have any umbrella except God. And that was good. Several churches became involved, so it was good there was no identity with a particular one. We found out later the Berean denomination heard about the camp and did want to sponsor it, but luckily Wendell and Marilyn prevented it.

"They were always telling people during the church services what was going on at camp, and had me share once in awhile. If you don't keep stoking the fire it's not going to work; they stoked it all the time. They know how many people have accepted the Lord at camps.

"Marilyn really got involved in helping with the food. She bought it and she cooked it. Then, like Sunday at their home, she had a breakfast, fourteen people for lunch, twelve people for supper, and then had a meeting with a missionary couple. Now I mean the church, the community, the camp…just everybody would be hurting without her.

"She served an eight-year term on the board and became chairman, I think in '97 or '98. I don't know how much the Sewards give, but it has been plenty. You know, people that have that vision and want to see something done, when there is a need they just give. I remember one time the camp was behind on the power bill and needed to do something about the water system. Well, there was no money, so Wendell and Marilyn took care of it. That's just them, that's all. You know how they are."

Pete became director of the camp in September of 1994. He explains, "It wasn't long before I learned that Marilyn had one basic pace, 'full speed ahead.' When there was a task to be done, if someone didn't volunteer right away, Marilyn would usually say, 'Oh, I can do it.' She was always meeting the need. She seems to gravitate toward projects others don't want to tackle. The more insurmountable the task the more she seems attracted to it. She usually works independently, probably because there are few that keep up with her pace, and then if she can do it, why bother other people? That can be good or bad.

"When I arrived it was not uncommon to see her car pull into the camp with the driver (her) barely visible in the surrounding groceries. The car was so full that when she'd open the doors something would usually fall out…maybe a pie or two. She would recruit friends to help with the cooking.

"It wasn't uncommon for the Sewards to have a family or two, or some foreign students, in their home while Marilyn was working at the camp. How she managed is a mystery to everybody.

"Obtaining the long-sought approval of the revised conditional use permit was ninety-five percent Marilyn's doing. This was no small deal. She worked on pushing it through for at least two years ('96, '97). She went personally to the county offices to get approval. I know she used more honey than vinegar. When the officials would come out to review the camp she would walk with them, letting them know she understood their concerns. When she didn't agree with something you could see it in her body language and then the psychology would start. She'd usually win, or at least get the better side of the compromise.

"Fund-raising was something Marilyn became excited about. She said she first saw most fund-raising as 'pushy religion' but later realized it was most often just sharing the needs and opportunities with those who seemed most interested in the particular ministry. She came to see responsible fund-raising as good stewardship involving sharing vision and opportunities."

Since its founding in the seventies to the present day, KCOC has steadily grown, now hosting several hundred campers and staff each summer. It is one of the notables of Scott Valley, with many churches near and far involved in supporting the camp, and supplying staff for the summers. The campers, mainly six through eighteen, come from a broad spectrum of society and distances.

Reaching kids with the Good News, and providing them with wholesome activities and contexts, has always been high on Marilyn and Wendell's priority list. Nowadays, with so many broken homes, the materialistic culture, and all the stuff that is thrown at them over the media and the Web (and in some schools), it is difficult for new generations to obtain a wholesome moral and ethical frame of reference for life. The Sewards' own experience has been testimony of how strategic a good camp program can be. It is an opportunity for both campers and staff to enjoy the outdoors and at the same time obtain a meaningful frame of reference built upon interpersonal relationships and biblical principles of loving care and truth, giving life meaning and hope.

Reflection

A wholesome investment in youth is a wise investment at any time. Each young person should understand he or she is their loving Creator's masterpiece...and they can reach for the stars...or, "what's a heaven for?" Children only get one shot at childhood. It needs to be meaningful and memorable. Christian camps minister in this vein.

When the Joneses had the vision to begin Kidder Creek Camp,
They found the Sewards eager to give their approval stamp;
Both couples' strong desire to see character built in kids,
Motivated them to work compassionately in everything they did

Chapter Eleven

Shepherds of the Valley

They're the Shepherds of the Valley, the tenders of the sheep,
They have Jesus as their resource, and drink from fountains deep;
Their compassion spans the valley, as the waters fill the sea,
Shoe-leather love's their method, reaching out to you and me.

"If international prizes are ever established for people in positive emotional involvement, Wendell and Marilyn Seward most certainly have to be at the top of the list."

This declaration appeared as the lead sentence under the June 18, 1980, Pioneer Press front page article banner: *The Shepherds of Our Valley*. It was accompanied by a picture of the couple standing on the deck of the cookhouse at Kidder Creek Orchard Camp where Marilyn was working as a cook for the summer. When Gary, Pioneer Press owner/editor, located them for the picture, it wasn't unexpected to find Marilyn at the camp. Wendell at the time was vice-president of the camp's advisory board.

By this time, the Sewards had been in Scott Valley for thirteen years. It is one thing for someone who knows the Sewards well to write a story about their lives. It is quite another for someone only casually familiar with them to be so impressed by positive emotional and spiritual tremors rippling across the valley to want to understand the cause and document the findings in public print. The tributaries of loving care were flowing from their lives to every community.

Shepherd...most everyone is familiar with the expression. The shepherd tends and cares for the flock. In this case the flock is "the valley" (and some beyond), and not just the church-goers. Wendell and Marilyn were involved in most aspects of valley life and culture.

The article goes on to say, "Hospitable ...shepherds of the church... kind...sensitive—are some of the ways many people who know the Sewards both in and out of the church speak of them. Although totally different in personality, Pastor Seward and his wife provide a complimentary effect on the community that makes them nearly impossible to separate.

"It would take a pair of parallel columns to chronicle their life achievements, most of which cannot even be measured in black and white terms.

"As of this spring it is Mayor Wendell of Etna, a job he slipped into with little fanfare, a job he could probably keep for as long a he wanted. Also a special education teacher in Yreka, Seward always seems to be on important committees in Scott Valley, keeping a low profile, a ready laugh and championing no particular cause, unless it be the underdog.

"Indeed, if one is looking for controversy in Wendell, it might be found only in his role as pastor. 'The congregation knows I make errors, that I'm not smooth, but I think that's why they relate to me.' Although his upbringing and the doctrine of the loosely knit Berean Church are 'theologically orthodox,' Wendell has departed from traditionalists in his 'open door' policy, drawing some of his standards from unusual sources.

'Both Marilyn and I now believe that we can accept someone and at the same time not approve of their behavior,' he said.

"The fifty-five-year-old pastor readily acknowledges that he has upset some of the conservative members of the congregation over his tendencies to 'accept everyone on face value.' To this point, in one sermon he told of a dignified man injured in an auto accident refusing to go to the hospital—where he was director—because he was without his medical insurance card, and because he was dirty and bloody. (He figured he would be ridiculed.)

'It occurs to me if a young person on a late Saturday night was run over by an unacceptable sin, the last place he or she would want to go would be his church. Can we be so holy as to not give love?'

"Marilyn Seward can only be described as a dynamo. Her husband calls her a person of 'extreme intelligence,' and notes that after thirty-three years of marriage she has never been anything but organized. Sunday was an example. Up early to bake six Father's Day pies for special people, she rushed to church where she taught an adult Sunday School class, played the organ, scampered home to serve lunch to a dozen guests and then dashed to Greenview Kidder Creek Camp where she almost single-handedly fixed an entire dinner for all the members of a soccer camp. Then it would usually be back to an evening meeting at the church, and no doubt later in the night entertaining the half dozen people who seem to filter into the couple's home from the church and neighborhood.

"She comments, 'Both Wendell and I are very fortunate, because people are our interest; they are the most important thing to us.' Asked how they coordinate their varying styles, Marilyn said, 'Any successful marriage has common goals, and we have those, particularly in helping people.' The fifty-two-year-old Mrs. Seward says the payoffs are evident. 'Seeing kids we've helped come back matured, living a ministry of their own, makes you feel like a little bit of your work has been multiplied.' However, some they admit haven't been success stories.

"Two of the most evident aspects of their 'team' approach are visible at home and in their counseling. Neighbors on the block might complain that the Sewards are running a boarding-house without proper zoning from outward signs. That is, they would if there were anyone else on the block. The three-story 'mansion' sits alone on a triangle of streets in a quiet residential area.

"During the past school year the Seward residence was 'home' for exchange students from Germany and Japan, a 'live-in' from the Salmon River, occasional short-term nurses working at the town's medical clinic, a temporarily displaced family waiting to re-occupy their house, and a various and assorted array of people passing in the night.

"But if the Sewards worried about the crowds you'd never guess it from talking to them. 'To me our house is the spirit of Scott Valley,' says Wendell. 'It's that instinctive trust, to help someone along the road.' But offering one of their four spare bedrooms isn't the limit of their efforts. Wendell and Marilyn are well known for their counseling skills.

"The joke in Oregon where they lived for seventeen years is, 'If you want comfort, go to Wendell; if you want help, go to Marilyn.' 'It's a most gratifying thing to see wholeness develop in families,' says Wendell. 'It's been a happy experience, a growing experience,' says Marilyn.

"A sentiment that could be echoed about the Sewards just as easily, particularly by nearly everyone who knows them." (End of article)

This article provides dimensions to the "Shepherds" theme. Twenty-seven years later a Yreka pastor would yet declare, "Wendell is the pastor...the master-shepherd of the county."

Reflection

The Seward's reputation was one of respect for all people, and of honor to the God of love and righteousness. They impacted nearly every segment of society with living examples of truth and love, guidance and healing. No one will deny their care-giving and servant posture --even those who may differ with them on some other points of belief or practice. In this way they take after the heart of Jesus, the "Great Shepherd."[1]

---

1   1 Peter 5:4

Chapter Twelve

Salt and De-light

---

*"While Europe has been guilty of keeping Jesus enshrined and America
has tended to incorporate Him, the Sewards have always attempted to
incarnate Him. This is wonderfully refreshing, like a drink from a pure
mountain stream. This is the essence of letting your body become the
temple of the Spirit of Jesus."*
Ken Needham, TransMission

When the Sewards run for public office it is almost "no contest." Loving and accepting people like they do, others sense they can be trusted unequivocally. People want them in positions of public responsibility. They've witnessed their servants' hearts and know they will not be self-serving but will act in the best interest of the community.

Marilyn states, "Wendell was elected mayor of Etna in March (1980) by an overwhelming, almost embarrassing, margin. He seems to really enjoy it. He continues to teach Special Ed (he just got his Special Ed credential), is on the medical board, and serves with the League of Cities. The county sheriff's department wants him to become the chaplain for the department. I think he'll do it. This means he'll have to ride with the deputies at times, and will need to be available for certain kinds of emergencies.

"I became a member of Women for Biblical Equality. I have felt strongly for years that the pendulum of women's issues and rights has swung too far one way or the other. The Bible, properly translated and understood, provides the balance God intended in His design of women and their roles in the Church and society. Much damage is done because many women are too suppressed, or, they want too many rights. Many problems in marriages and families would never occur if women understood and lived the life our Creator designed for them. Of course, men also need to understand the biblical view, not just women. If that doesn't happen, then the problems will never go away.

"After a tough year, things are going well at Quartz Valley School for me. We have sixty kids, an excellent staff, and a brand-new classroom we'll use for French, music, and rainy-day P.E. Oh…I have to be there by seven a.m. to build the two wood fires. That's our old-fashioned touch.

"I've just reread all our Christmas letters since 1959…marveling at God's goodness…also realizing why Wendell is this minute in Chico taking a course in Stress Management! I'm hearing 'feelers' about another four years on city council…he's served twelve already. He does enjoy being mayor! I'm more aware of his perception in spiritual things; in some ways, he's years ahead of his time. He still works harder at being a good husband than anyone else I know!" Marilyn wrote this in December 1981.

Wendell was then riding the crest of a ripple that later became a wave going into the 21st century. Churches were beginning to realize their impact upon society was weak. Institutionalized Christianity had a predominant culture that was too confined within its own walls, and was either alienated or ignored by most of the unchurched. George Barna, an accomplished Christian market researcher/analyst, was giving warnings through books and other publications that the Church overall was losing its transformational impact on society, and that it was being plagued by the same humanistic and materialistic corrosion that was eroding the nation's morals.[1]

Wendell's stance regarding church and humanity was based upon serving, loving, and accepting. He desired the Church to manifest these attributes to all spectrums of society, and especially to the poor and marginalized. He taught "look up" (in dependence and worship) not "out" (in criticism and judgment). His premise was the Church (Christ-followers) should always be the serving community—serving the community. The local gatherings were not to produce spectators, but participants embracing all ages and types. He and Marilyn were strong ambassadors for God's purpose to seek and save the lost. They really didn't fit any of the denominational boxes—not even their own. To them, when believers came together it was a time of joy and freedom, sharing blessings, needs and spiritual gifts, praise and worship…and usually some teaching. They

---

1 Barna Research Group, or, The Barna Group, www.barna.org

wanted a non-religious atmosphere where everyone would feel welcome and could participate if they desired.

One particular anecdote illustrates the atmosphere of freedom in their church. Bill Birch and Wendell spoke on alternate months at the Berean church. Bill was speaking one Sunday morning and made the observation, "As you are well aware we all have a sex drive..." He no sooner got the words out when Julia, one of the church founders now in her eighties hollered, "*Not any more!*" Well, pandemonium followed and a giggle now and then was heard throughout the morning. Bill was finally able to finish his thought...then to cap it off, the next week, just before he went up to speak, he snuck behind Julia and looped a big red bandana around her head so it covered her mouth, and knotted it in the back. It was awhile before the crowd calmed down and Bill could get enough composure to speak. Julia, not to be outdone, re-tied the bandana around her head in "hippie-style."

Stuff like that happened on a regular basis. Wendell and Bill played a continual game of "one-upmanship" on each other in the "trick and tease" department. Sometimes, Wendell would dress up like some historical character who he was going to mention in his teaching, and this usually brought a few teasing hoots. I can still see him in his long wool overcoat and fedora as he was bringing a message featuring William Wilberforce, the great British abolitionist and Christian statesman of two hundred years ago. Hunching a bit, and swinging his arms in broad gestures (very unlike himself), he pleaded the cause of freedom and human rights as did Wilberforce before Parliament. It was a masterful and memorable grace-based message.[2]

Around this time, Marilyn relates, "While I play college student, Wendell-the-Mayor is discovering that swimming pools, upgraded water/sewage systems and dog control ordinances do not make everyone equally happy...but he still loves the job. I would love to watch him in action in a council meeting. "One of our 'sunshine pools' this year was Ken Medema's concert. Although Ken is blind he, like Helen Keller, sees more than most people. He gives us a short piano concert in the

---

2   William Wilberforce's life was featured in the film, <u>Amazing Grace</u>, released in 2007.

morning; sits through the rest of the service; comes to our yard to eat lunch and chat with a crowd of people; and then in the evening provides a remarkable concert, actually capturing in his lyrics many of the happenings of the day, and giving keen insights into the things he has *seen*. He is incredible in his talent, and such a tenderhearted, precious man of God. We all just love him, and he promises he will return.

"I just finished my last exam for my Master's degree and administrative credential. What a long haul that's been—literally—this fall, as a fellow teacher and I drove each Tuesday after school to Chico, two hundred miles away, attended class, drove home to bed at two a.m., and up again at six a.m. for school. But I'm through now—JOY! When I finished my thesis/project and oral exam this summer, MeriJean threw a big surprise party for one hundred and thirty friends to celebrate her mom's achievement." Significant healing has taken place in mom and MeriJean's relationship!

The summer of 1985, Wendell and Marilyn spent nearly six weeks in Europe. Taking a cruise down the Rhine, they were in awe of the ancient castles on the various promontory points. Then their long-anticipated experience: they saw the Passion Play in Oberammargau, Germany, an extravaganza and moving spiritual experience. The web site explains, "More than 2,000 Oberammergauers, actors, singers, instrumentalists and stage technicians bring to the stage in approximately six hours of playing time, those events Christianity regards as its central source of life and hope "

The last fifteen days of the trip, using their Eurail Pass, they visited nine exchange students who had lived with them and others in the valley. Marilyn said, "Hardly a day passes without us recalling some happy memory of our summer. Contrary to predictions, we returned home refreshed, not exhausted! And surprise! While we were gone our 'resident family' and neighbors surprised us with finishing our third floor and installing a skylight. We hired a teacher at Quartz Valley with a music credential the day before school started. I had to scratch some of my own pay to afford her. So now I am a principal 'for nothing.' Wendell has another great sixth grade class, continues to enjoy his mayoral and civic duties, and reached his *sixtieth* birthday in September with no special effort on his part!"

✛ ✛ ✛

Wendell enjoyed teaching his Special Ed class. He was well known for his rapport with the kids. I was talking to fellow teacher, Macy Smith, in their hilltop home overlooking beautiful Shasta Valley back-dropped by the imposing fourteen-thousand-foot Mount Shasta.

She shared, "Wendell is a very special person. He conducted my mother's funeral and the weddings for both my son and my daughter. I subbed for Wendell quite a bit during the Eighties. I subbed for him when he broke his foot on the playground playing with the kids. The week he was out I had a steady stream of students, current and former, coming into the room to ask me how he was doing. Remarkable…they were so fond of him.

"One girl came in and said, 'I'm not very pretty.' She was about thirteen. She said, 'Mr. Seward told me every young girl has her time to be beautiful, whether it's eleven or twelve or eighteen. I hope some day I might look pretty.' She was rather plain looking. Four or five years later I saw her on a float in the Homecoming parade. She was strikingly beautiful! It was so thoughtful of Wendell to do that. It gave her such hope.

"Our son, Tom, had a hard time in school. He had no self confidence. Wendell helped Tom in a remarkable way in the sixth grade. The teachers he had before didn't really help him. Wendell built him up and the difference seemed like a miracle. Wendell gave him confidence in himself and this turned his life around. He did that for a lot of kids. Tom is now number five in the nation as salesman for Sun Belt, a big equipment rental company.

"Wendell always got the troubled kids in his class. A superintendent told me Wendell turned troubled kids around when no one else could. He loved the kids and made them feel good about themselves, and that was the difference. I don't think he mixed with the teachers too well. It's hard to explain. We teachers are a funny group. Many like to think they're the best teacher in school. Some of them were a little jealous of Wendell. He helped some of the kids they couldn't. He was teaching for the right reasons.

"More recently, Marilyn mentored my daughter when she was starting to teach here in Yreka. Marilyn drove over from Etna, I think twice a week, all on her own time. She's a master teacher and has a caring heart. My daughter can't say enough good things about her.

"I am so thankful this book is being written. People like the Sewards are model citizens. They make such a big difference for the better wherever they go. They are wonderful examples of what unselfish love can accomplish in this world. They are so humble and don't put on airs. The world needs a lot more people like Wendell and Marilyn."

Marilyn has some interesting reflections on year 1985. "This year has not gone according to any careful plan. In fact, a lot of plans had to be scrapped! In March, Wendell had prostate surgery; the doctor found a trace of cancer. He spent a much quieter spring and summer than usual, even though he did perform an outdoor wedding in a foot of snow one week after his surgery! He's fine now, and enjoying still another delightful sixth grade class. He almost missed his sixty-first birthday party due to funerals—four in one week. Even with weddings, counseling, city council/mayoral duties and all the rest, he still finds time to watch Nebraska or Baylor football on TV. When he walks down for the mail on Saturdays, I know it could be three hours before he returns; there are just so many people to visit!"

Regarding church life in the valley, there were some good things taking place. Marilyn explains, "With three new younger pastors in Scott Valley (Methodist, CMA, and Village Missions), all warm and caring, and the dedicated Adventist couple plus a wonderful Catholic priest, the spiritual climate has changed significantly from what it was when we came nineteen years ago. We pastoral families all get together once a month for potluck and sharing. We still sense we are onlookers as 'God moves in mysterious ways His wonders to perform.'"

In late January of 1988 Judi and I had moved our families from Pasadena, California, to Etna, lock, stock and barrel. Our caravan included Judi's mom and dad, ourselves and our two boys, Stephen and David, then ten and three. "Grandma"—Judi's mom—was miraculously recovering from a decade-long illness and this started a new era for her. Our dear friend, Armin McKee, came to Pasadena to move us in his Peterbilt semi, and that long trailer was jammed full to the roof. We had been in Pasadena for nearly five years, where we started Global Mapping International (GMI).[3] In addition to both families' belongings, we moved GMI's global headquarters, furniture, and files, to Etna.

Why Etna? It's hard to pin down all of the reasons, but three stand out. *First,* we had friends in the valley we had met through Overseas Crusades Family Conferences at Mount Hermon Christian Conference Center over the years. In '72 we had met Bill and Marilyn Coe, ranchers living in a nearby valley. The next year we met the Sewards, and began a warm relationship with them, dropping in on them and the Coes from time to time.

Second, we thought it would be a desirable environment for raising our boys, Stephen and David. Stephen was already in the fifth grade. During visits we checked out the schools and found them top-notch.

Third, we had been living with Judi's folks for five years. Judi's mom had needed her daughter's constant care and now that she was healed, we felt they would really enjoy the quiet and beauty of the rural mountain setting: the pine trees, green fields, crystal lakes, and wildlife. It worked out that way. It was a blessing to hear grandpa in the woods with his chainsaw cutting up fallen dead trees for firewood, and to see grandma planting flowers or hear her beautiful voice charming the foxes or deer in the meadow. I was traveling a lot overseas in those days and was comforted to know the family was happy, secure, and surrounded by caring friends.

That first evening after a day of unpacking, Judi and I found ourselves sitting on a grassy slope with Wendell, watching a musical comedy, the "Cotton Patch Gospel," at the Britt Festival in nearby Jacksonville, Oregon. He and Marilyn had seen it just the night before and he thought it was so good it would be a good way for us to relax. He was right. The hilarious show was great therapy. It was the first time I had heard Judi roar with a belly-laugh and we'd been married sixteen years! A wonderful launch into a new era in our lives. On our way back home Wendell was telling us a little about himself and Marilyn, and kiddingly said, "*Marilyn and I get along fine, but she is pretty much her own woman and knows what she wants. She'll ask me my opinion, but I know what she really wants is to hear her own opinion in a lower voice.*" We had another good laugh.

---

3   Nine years after starting Global Mapping, the Waymires moved to Etna, California where they started LIGHT International, a research and strategy consultancy for global missions.

So there you pretty much have it. We moved because of the relationship with friends, good schools, and the slower pace and beauty of a rural/mountain environment. From the first week after we moved in January of 1988, Wendell and I started having a weekly breakfast together. We met at six-thirty a.m. at Bob's Ranch House, because Wendell had to then drive the twenty-six miles to Yreka where he was teaching. In 1993, when Wendell and Marilyn both retired from teaching, it became the four of us every Tuesday morning at Bob's—but at a more relaxing eight a.m. rather than six-thirty.

I was counting one day, and that's when I discovered that Wendell and I have had nearly nine hundred bowls of oatmeal or multi-grain cereal over the years—and he ate all my raisins. We terrorized our share of waitresses over the years, and looked forward to Tuesdays every week! (I remember one Tuesday, after breakfast with the Sewards. Wendell told a corny joke and Marilyn sighed, "Oh brother." We heard that response from her many times, but it didn't deter Wendell nor bother us. We'd always have to smile). Oh…the joke ?

"When I'm on my death bed I would like to have an IRS agent on one side of the bed, and my lawyer friend, Mark, on the other." And one of us asked, "Why is that?" "Well, that way I'd be like Jesus and die between two criminals." (Yes…"oh brother!")

Reflection

With the Sewards, light was not hid under a basket, nor salt confined to the shaker. They drink life from a big cup; big enough to share generously with others. Positive reinforcement produces marvelous results. Others are beneficiaries of the Spirit's transforming work within these two people. And for many, Marilyn and Wendell were shining stars; guiding lights in the darkness.

Wedding Party with Marilyn and Wendell – June 1947

Wendell – wartime – 23

Marilyn in Iowa – 18

Wendell and Marilyn in Etna – June 1980
Headline Picture "Shepherds of our Valley."

The Shepherds at home – 2006

Marilyn far right, first row – Windy Summit School, Essex, Iowa -1937

The Sewards with 'live-ins' in the 70's. All are now leading successful lives.

Marilyn (far right) and child-care team at an
International Conference in 2000, Canterbury, England.

Marilyn with Scott Valley staff,
Canterbury, England

Marilyn and Olympic torch -
England conf. 2000

Scott Valley Berean Church Sewards were the first pastors - 1967 until 2001

Quartz Valley School 10 miles from Etna. Marilyn taught here from
1967 to 1993 when she retired. During this time she also became
principal and superintendent.

Marilyn and Wendell; daughter MeriJean and son David
Taken at 60th wedding anniversary

Three generations of Seward men - Cameron, Wendell, David

"Pastor Wendell Seward from Etna officiated at the karaoke wedding ceremony of clowns James Parks and Ruth McCready at a noon wedding at the
Weed 'Carnevale'. He was possibly the only one on the stage that didn't sing.
"Serious, yet humorous, could well describe the wedding. The informality
of Pastor Seward's remarks brought times of laughter while the serious-
ness of his message about permanent commitment and love kept the event
grounded.' *Love is something you do, not feel. Love is doing something for the
other person.' Seward said. 'God gave a gift and wrapped it in a person. This is
a divine gift. Don't desecrate it.'"*

Chapter Thirteen

Testing, Testing

"I was tired of Christian leaders using biblical principles to protect their power, to draw a line in the sand separating the good army from the bad one...I wondered whether any human being could be an enemy of God..."
Donald Miller, *Blue Like Jazz* [1]

The turn of the century saw the Sewards functioning adroitly in their multi-tasking world. They had in mind to retire from church leadership at some not-too-distant point, but at the same time there were some troubling indications that a new staff member plus some elders wanted to lead the Scott Valley church in a different direction. The Sewards were concerned it was a "reversal in direction" back into the realm of traditional religious institutions, with the emphasis on knowledge and structure...and adherence to denominational doctrine.

With the clouds darkening, we might expect the Sewards to become somewhat discouraged and debilitated, especially when they had labored so hard for the church to become relational, freedom-loving and non-religious. The church had always been admired in the community for its "open arms" policy, its freedom and joy, and the fact that the Sewards accepted one and all without discrimination, and with special compassion for the poor and downtrodden. Now they were beginning to see the "handwriting on the wall" as a measure of control and formality was taking shape with a noticeable impact on the joy and freedom of the Spirit.

The blow finally came: a letter from the board outlining a new structure and new direction that the Sewards could not, in all good

---

1   pp 216, 221 (*Blue Like Jazz*)

conscience, go along with. It would mean reversing thirty years of hard-won change. They submitted their letter of resignation to the board.

Wendell and Marilyn were deeply wounded. They had some sleep-less nights and times of pain and anguish, especially when they thought about all the people who were just coming into the knowledge that they are valuable to God, that He loves them deeply, and that they can love others with that same love—no matter their actions or station in life.

At the end of the year, Marilyn, with her objectivity intact, put this light on it: "In February, after two tough years, Wendell and I submit-ted our resignation to the church, realizing we just couldn't support the direction the church board wanted to assume. We have been quietly searching for next steps; so far, no blazing light! In the meantime, we are doing what we have always done. Both of us continue all the volunteer work (about ten different groups between the two of us), Wendell has preached at several other churches, had lots of weddings and funerals, spent hours in care-giving, counseling, and helping the helpless."

Wendell had been speaking periodically for Mike Yaconelli at a Church in Yreka, which met at the Grange Hall. Upon his learning of the Sewards' situation, Mike and Karla immediately invited them to become involved in leading the services at Grace. The Yaconellis were very understanding and empathetic to their situation, and held them both in high regard.

Wendell and Marilyn, accepting the invitation, soon left the Etna church and started at Grace Community. This turn of events obviously grieved the spirit of the Berean church and many in the community. The mission people in the church still looked to Marilyn for leader-ship in missions, and of course she responded whole-heartedly. This seemed to be fine with everybody. The fact they didn't miss a beat in ministering in the community and beyond testifies to a high level of spiritual maturity, commitment, and humility.

This whole church situation, sadly, is repeated in many communi-ties in many countries. It is too common a malady. Harold Bell Wright, an author of a century ago, had keen spiritual insight regarding this condition. *The Calling of Dan Matthews*[2] is a story describing the pre-ponderance of churches in our day—and, in fact, in every day:

2   Harold Bell Wright, *The Calling of Dan Matthew* (New York, A.L. Burt Co., 1909). Recently re-published under   the title, A Higher Call

"…Dan broke forth in a laugh, such a laugh as the Doctor had never heard from his lips. 'Believe…respect! Then why do they allow it to go on?'

"'Because,' said the old man, 'it is their religion to worship an institution, not a God; to serve a system, not the race of men. They do not know they are doing it, of course. They think all their religious affairs and their church programs are signs of true faith. They have no idea they are just worshipping an institution, a club, a social organization. That's what makes it so lethal, because they see none of it. It is history, my boy. Every reformation begins with the persecution of the reformer and ends with the followers of that reformer persecuting those who would lead them another step toward freedom. It happens in great movements, it happens in small church settings, but it is always the same. When someone tries to implement change against the grain of the status quo—what our Lord called the "traditions of the elders"—they will be chewed up and spit out. Misguided religious people have always crucified their saviors and always will!'

"Dan was silent. He had never seen this side of the Doctor, so perceptive about spiritual things. He found himself awed by the revelation of his old friend's mind.

"Presently the Doctor continued. 'There is no hatred, lad, so bitter as that hatred born of a religious love. There is no falsehood so vile as the lie spoken in defense of truth. There is no wrong so harmful as the wrong committed in the name of righteousness, no injustice so terrible as the injustice of those who condemn in the name of the Savior of the world.'

"'What then, as you see it—what can I do?' asked Dan.

Wright, through the old doctor, insightfully describes the subtle chemistry that has remained active in the organized Church since the first Christian led the Roman Empire and infused into the fourth century Church's DNA a mix of pagan and Christian principles, values and practices. This phenomenon has plagued the Body of Christ these many centuries. The Reformation saw some reform in certain facets of theology, but the Church structure remained mostly intact.

Many church-goers will have a hard time with the above characterization by Wright, but as a way of test, they might ask themselves how

guilty they would feel if they missed a Sunday or they did not want
to obey what a church "officer" told them to do. Tradition is deeply
ingrained and holds more power over us than we might realize. Many
people hear the Word, but few are those who do it. (James 1:22-25)

The Etna church, growing in health and vitality for thirty-three
years, experiences an attack of what is increasingly being called "traditional church disease."

The Sewards leaving the church brought literally dozens of questions
and comments, and when queried regarding why they left the church,
they would say they felt they needed to resign as others wanted to take
leadership. And when pushed for details they would respond, "It's a
long story…too complicated to explain." It is impossible to know all
the rumors that may have been floating about, or how many of them
were true.

When Kathy and Gary Opfer, missionaries in Croatia and Kosovo
and who had once lived in Etna, heard of the Seward-church situation, Kathy wrote, "This is Wendell's greatest testing. He has invested
in loving and caring for and accepting and forgiving people most of
his life. Now some of those closest to him seem to have betrayed him.
The real test now is to see if he can forgive them, and accept them, and
not condemn them. This is probably the biggest test of all, for these are
Christians. This is a serious time in the Sewards' life. They have given
so much of themselves to others, and most of the rest of us just admire
them but can't seem to repeat what they do at the level they do it. And
then in the midst of this lack of understanding they get persecuted and
pushed out. Yes, this will be their biggest test yet."

I was talking to Dick and Norma Jones (founders) about the history of Kidder Creek Orchard Camp, a few months after the Sewards
had left the Etna church, and Dick said, "Now I know you didn't come
to talk about this, but I'd like to say one other thing. This thing that
happened at church…I feel sorry for Wendell because I know he must
feel some rejection, but he has to let it go. You can't change your yester-
days. He can't let the root of bitterness into his heart. The guys on the
board don't know what they're doing. They're too young. And maybe
Wendell isn't the best teacher around, but he's still the most respected

and most effective. But Wendell's temperament is so sensitive. He has such great gifts even though he doesn't know it. There's nobody who has his grace and compassion. Just like the baptism yesterday or the funeral last week. Nobody does them like Wendell. I hope he doesn't let this church thing ruin all that. I really don't think he will. Marilyn will help him. But we all need to keep him in our prayers."

Reflection

It is hazardous business to bear the torch into the dark and infected recesses where men hide their selfishness and misconceptions. Wendell left to others the credit of expounding and defending the more popular themes of scripture and religious creeds. His speech didn't have the embroidery of some, but the fabric was substantial, serving life's truest purposes. We would all be safe in emulating the zeal and compassion with which both Sewards labored for the public good, and the fortitude with which they endured trials and sufferings.

The gathering making up Grace Community Church in Yreka is quite unique. Many attending would not attend a traditional church. Grace Community is anything but traditional, and this suits the Sewards and everyone else splendidly. Many who attend participate in the service one way or another. A break is taken during the service for coffee and goodies. The overall atmosphere is one of informality and freedom. There is structure, but it isn't rigid. The first Sunday of each month, the down-to-earth Nazarene pastor brings a message, then heads to his own church.

Some years back I was sitting next to a middle-aged woman who had just been released from jail the night before. About half way through the meeting when Mike Yaconelli was speaking, she leaned over to me and whispered, *"This is where us misfits fit."* It made Mike's and the Sewards' day.

Guillermo, from Spain, who had lived with the Sewards as an exchange student in the nineties, recently (August 2007) returned for a visit. He attended Grace one Sunday and near the end of the meeting said, "This is a church for people who don't like church."

One time, Mike, going on longer than usual, said finally, "There's just one more point..." Sadie, a sweetie with Down's Syndrome, moaned quite loudly, "Oh no!" Everyone laughed and Mike said, "I didn't realize I was through...but I am."

I loved the fact that it wasn't my responsibility to change somebody, it was God's, my part was just to communicate love and approval... I ask God to make it so both conversations, this one from the mouth and the one from the heart, are true."
Donald Miller, *Blue Like Jazz*

Chapter Fourteen

Love in Action

"A commitment that is not visible in human service,
suffering discipleship, and creative love, is an illusion."
Brennan Manning[1]

With the Sewards there was always a life-giving stew abrew, and thus it continued through the years. As you wander through the hills and valleys of this chapter, you may be puzzled as to why this couple involved themselves in so many things. I believe the Apostle Paul described it when he said, "The love of Christ controls us."[2] I believe this exactly fits the Sewards. Contemplating lost and wounded souls actually pains them. Watching people be persecuted and put down wounds them. Seeing people led astray by false teaching hurts them. Being unable to meet many of the vital needs they see haunts them. Helping people gain victory over problems energizes them.

Wendell served as county sheriff's chaplain for a number of years, and performed weddings for many of the deputies. He rode with them from time to time, finding himself in a number of extraordinary situations.

"Sometimes they'd pick me up at seven o'clock in the evening, and we'd be gone until four o'clock in the morning. In one situation we spotted a girl in downtown Etna who was on probation for drug abuse and was under observation. The deputy got out and began to

1   Brennan Manning, *Abba's Child: The Cry of the Heart for Intimate Belonging* (Colorado Springs, NavPress, 1994) p.143
2   Second Corinthians 5:14

ask some questions and she started to run. When he stopped her, she
said she was pregnant and that he was upsetting her. She didn't want
him to touch her because he might cause her to have a miscarriage.
The deputy called for a female deputy, and wanted the girl to wait in
the car. She started pounding on him so he cuffed her and put her in
the front seat. I was in the back seat. She got pretty wild and kicked
out the windshield! When the female deputy arrived, the girl decided
she wasn't pregnant after all, but said the deputy had hurt her back. I
knew better.

"One reason they like me along is I provide a witness. They ended
up taking her to the station, booking her, and later releasing her. Some
days later I saw her in Etna and stopped to talk. I asked if I could give
her a hug? She said, 'Yes,' then said, 'Sometimes that's the best medicine there is.' I never mentioned that night, and she and I have been
friends ever since. You know, so many people like that are really good
people, they've just been dealt a bad hand from society.

"Another time, the sheriff's department called and asked me to
go the heliport. There was a family whose husband/father had died
on the trail to Spirit Lake and they were bringing them down by helicopter. (I had a strange feeling about this because a couple of years
before I had spent time with a family where the wife had died in
Spirit Lake and they never found her.) A medic had been flown in by
highway patrol helicopter but it arrived too late. The man had died
of a heart attack and fallen into a stream. When the chopper brought
the family out, I was there to meet them. They were having a hard
time. I bought the fifteen-year-old daughter a drink from a machine
and we had a good talk. She was very mature. The group needed a
place to stay so I took them to the Amerihost Hotel in Yreka (18
miles distant), got two rooms and gave them money for food. They
were really thankful."

Wendell seldom missed a Rotary meeting and would share there from
time to time. He was active in the Siskiyou County Pastoral Committee, with more tenure than any other pastor, as well as the Siskiyou
Domestic Violence Council. Regarding his presence there Marilyn observed, "He's their only pastoral representative; this has involved some

very special counseling which has opened our eyes to a world of unbelievable violence. Wendell helped get a grant for leasing a large house here in Etna just two blocks from our home, where battered spouses and other victims could live and have care. Wendell and I spent a lot of time counseling there. His roles with the behavioral health, the sheriff's chaplaincy, the jail and hospital visits caused him to be well known in the courts as an advocate for those who have messed up and don't know how to get un-messed. He's well known in most of the public offices."

A ministry Wendell has loved is officiating at weddings and funerals, making himself available as often as possible. Marilyn is involved in the majority of them held in the valley. She has a team of women who just "do it" (baby showers as well). Over the years, they became experts at flower arrangements, finger foods and table settings.

Wendell wouldn't usually accept any remuneration for the weddings, saying, "Why should I put a burden on them when I enjoy it so much? It is a gift from me to them." He's held weddings in interesting places, such as jails, logging camps, carnivals, several different states, and a few foreign countries. He'd make the occasions light-hearted and warm, always finding something relating to the couple and their family's personal lives to include in the program, sprinkling the ceremony with humor when appropriate and talking about the need for willing mutual commitment, submission and accountability to make the marriage work (and he'd extend this commitment to include family and friends). Because of the length of time he and Marilyn taught school, many of their previous students have had Wendell perform their ceremonies.

Joe, an old-time rancher in the area, approached Wendell after he spoke at the memorial service for widely known and admired cowboy Bob Axton. "Wendell, I just wanted to let you know ever since you folks came here and got involved in all the things you do and started that Berean church, this valley has been changed for the better."

"Uh...well, thanks, Joe."

Wendell was nearly speechless. Joe didn't attend church... never had, as far as he knew.

Margie, a Christian, made a similar comment. "The spiritual atmosphere of this valley has changed since you folks have been here." I've heard statements similar to this for several years. People, whether Christian or not, sense a difference. What is it?

In Garden of Eden parlance, they don't eat from the Tree of the Knowledge of Good and Evil, but from the Tree of Life.[3] The former tree provides food for the intellect too often used as a frame of reference for judgment and criticism. The sad part is, we too often use this knowledge of good and evil as a source of justification for our actions. We turn the New Testament into a Law—that kills. The Tree of Life provides nourishment for the heart, a heart that doesn't get turned off or intimidated by any of the subtle or atrocious acts mankind falls into, but takes initiative in reaching out to people—all people; a heart that meets judgment with an opposite spirit, the spirit of forgiveness and love.

Wendell and Marilyn's involvement in the community put them in contact with a wide variety of people. Many people were in their home. People began to adopt and replicate their non-judgmental, loving, accepting attitudes. The Holy Spirit was working. Jesus' loving care was penetrating and transforming attitudes in the valley. The Sewards were making a vital catalytic contribution to these dynamics.

There are so many "life stories" that could be told from the lives touched by the Sewards. Whether briefly or extensively, all who came in touch with them were changed—profoundly. Here are the words of Bo Bottomly—*Colonel* Bo Bottomly—whose life course, like so many others, was profoundly altered as a result of time spent in the loving care of the Sewards.

Bo[4] was born in 1919 in Montana. He has had an illustrious and adventurous career, mainly in the Air Force, including serving a stint as Secretary to the Joint Chiefs of Staff. He has shared many of his adventures via books, CDs, DVDs and film.

"Just out of the Air Force, I was driving north, heading back home to Montana, with everything I owned in my pickup truck. I was looking for a gas station with cheap gas and a place to spend the night. Near Yreka, California, I drove over a pass to Etna where I found a station and filled up there. It was dark so I slept in the back of my truck. It was Saturday night.

"The next morning was Sunday and so I found a church, and Wendell recognized me from my movie. He introduced himself and made

---

3   See Genesis Chapter 2 verse 8 thru Chapter 3 verse 7
4   Colonel Bo Bottomly is a decorated flyer having flown a variety of aircraft in many different theatres in four different wars. At one point he was Secretary to the Joint Chiefs of Staff. A premier story-teller, he has recorded most of his life in daily journals. See http://www.colonelbowar-stories.com/about_bo_bottomly.html

me feel welcome. I think Marilyn asked me to come over to Sunday dinner, like she does with everybody (half of whom are vagrants, like me). We just got to be friends, and Wendell told me that if I didn't have any place to go (and I indicated I didn't), that I could stay in a house next to the church until I decided what I wanted to do. I had told him I was recovering from an alcohol problem. I soon found lots of friends who kind of shepherded me and helped me along; however, my main relationship was with Wendell and Marilyn and whoever was around their home, usually exchange students and a few others.

"The Sewards were about the only real friends I had back then. Of course the church people were friendly. I couldn't believe it! It was such an open, friendly, forgiving place. And at times I shared the troubles I was having and no one poured salt in my wounds. When you're recovering from alcohol, you get into all sorts of mental snarls because your brain doesn't know quite how to figure it out. You keep turning things over to God and then grabbing them back. You think you're sinking and not swimming, and it's just a very confusing, difficult time.

"Marilyn and Wendell helped in amazingly opposite ways. Wendell was very comforting and soothing and compassionate, but Marilyn was almost the opposite. She would recognize the phony junk I was talking and tell me it was phony. She was very straight and very unforgiving about some of my attitudes and some of my behavior and some of my selfish ways of expressing myself. So the two of them were kind of like, 'good cop, bad cop' for getting me healed. And the way it worked, I received nothing but good.

"Wendell was chairman of the Youth and Children Committee for the North County for awhile and I was kind of his assistant up in the valley. He was just about to retire, and having spent a long time as a sixth grade school teacher, you'd think he'd be fed up with kids. It was amazing how compassionate he was and how fascinated he was in helping the unfortunate young people that were in trouble. Mainly because of economic problems, some of the families couldn't afford to have their kids checked or examined or treated for minor psychological or mental aberrations.

"In the early '90s he and Marilyn both retired, freeing up a lot of their time, so Wendell spent almost all his spare time worrying about, thinking about, and acting on kids around sixth-grade age, many of them with special needs. I think Wendell was the one who had a han-

dle on it and most people didn't. He understands how powerful acceptance and love and positive encouragement are at that critical age.

"I think one of Wendell's greatest strengths as a preaching pastor
was that he would make people think. He didn't necessarily entertain
Christians who didn't seem to be moving or growing in loving and
accepting people. Most all of his sermons were Bible-centered and
would be like in Matthew where Jesus said, 'You've heard it said to
love your friends and hate your enemies, but I say to you love your
enemies, do good to those that revile and trouble you.' That was a
very revolutionary thought and most people didn't really think Jesus
was serious. But it was such a major, giant step in love to include not
only people you don't know, but your *enemies*! I think Wendell had
caught on to and lived the tolerant, compassionate love that Jesus
was speaking about when he made the statement that Matthew recorded.

"I think Wendell's biggest value was that he kept on the very edge
of being almost unbelievable. You couldn't really believe that he was
seriously advocating something because it was something that only
Jesus would say. And everybody tried to avoid it after that. I think a
lot of his sermons were right on the edge of people waking up in their
hearts and thinking, *I wonder if you could really do that? I wonder if
you could really practice that? Really love people unconditionally?* But
they could see it was possible because Wendell lived it himself...most
of the time. That's what he is known for.

"Most of the major pharisaic high church people, including many
church leaders today, don't really function like that. So much has
changed from Jesus' time, but it shouldn't. Wasn't it Mahatma Ghandi
of India who said, 'I like your Jesus, but I don't like you Christians.'? We
all know why, don't we?

"Marilyn was a classic example of a mother. She was always giving counsel and helping and guiding and keeping people on the right
track. She even mothered me through part of my recovery. She would
give me advice as if I were a small child and I'd take it like that, usually.
Sometimes I wouldn't.

"Usually she was kind enough and right enough that I was willing.
And she always had a bunch of people in the house...from different
walks of life. Some were foreign exchange students. Sometimes they'd
come over from the Forks of Salmon. And the Sewards didn't care if

they were church people or not. They always had people staying there who they were helping get on their feet and get started again.

"I think Marilyn's real value was that there seemed to be no end to her energy for helping people. I don't know...she must be in her seventies. She is still a bundle of energy, always looking for somebody who needs help and making a bunch of telephone calls, getting the resources, organizing the people who are going to be involved, transportation or whatever it is to get the job done.

"And she's very, very sensitive to the slightest sound in the distance of somebody who needs help of some sort. And she is always organizing others, or getting the funds, or getting the food, or getting the clothing, or getting the blankets and doing something about all kinds of stuff. And she always answers the telephone with great courtesy and warmth and enthusiasm.

"They both believe the Christian community is not only a spiritual connection but a sociological connection as well. They are both involved in social issues and also in political issues and troubles and difficulties, and they are absolutely honest about what they think. They don't hedge. Neither one of them would hedge or rationalize or explain; if they think something is wrong, they just say it...but with love.

"A little backwoods valley like ours, kind of hidden away from civilization, can get awfully ingrown and inbred with our thoughts as well as our spiritual lives unless there's an inflow of ideas that are new and stimulating. The Sewards are very conscious of that. I think the fact they were teachers helped them to realize that. They are very avid readers and they always are into everything, new ideas and new thoughts."

Bo's words could be echoed by hundreds of other people. But it's also revealing that Bo, like so many others, sees Marilyn as this invincible dynamo, this super-human fount of energy and action; so much so that we, and she, sometimes forget that we are all human, that we all have our limits, and that we must at times either seek help, or even let others "do it" when it becomes too much for us. As the years passed, Marilyn could not always keep up the incredible pace she set for herself—no one could. And this finally became apparent one day during the service at Grace Community Church.

Marilyn lost it. It wasn't a traumatic thing...well, not very. It just seemed so out of character for her. She was leading the first song and it didn't seem familiar to her, which was strange. She was having trouble with the timing and melody. At the end of the verse she was a little flustered. She took off her glasses and looked at them like they were the problem. Then she shook her head and we sang the second verse. It seemed to be going a little better, but when the singing stopped she made an awkward pause.

Standing with glasses in hand, her face anguished, she said haltingly, "I've had a terrible time these last few days. I had this long, complicated grant proposal I had to prepare relating to a water project for Etna, and I had a deadline to send the form in by Friday to the West Coast Watershed office in Yreka. I finished it Friday and tried to send it via email and the office called and said the forms came through all blank...and there were many pages. They are so long and complicated, and I can barely understand them.

"Then I tried to send some things and the attachments didn't make it. I really need some help. Would you please pray for me, that I would be able to get the right help and to work through this?" (Her eyes were very moist.)

You could feel the empathy reaching out from all of us. This was a seldom-seen Marilyn. She's always been the dynamo, the capable one, the "Katie-bar-the-door" person.

It is significant she felt the freedom to share this...to open herself up and let people see her frustration and her weakness; to see her in a state of need.

She felt secure there among her friends. Over the years at Grace, she had witnessed to a lot of hurting people, many of whom had the courage to share things people normally are afraid to share. Now they were really reaching out to her, with true empathy.

That's one of the things we like about the *Grace* Community. You can lose it and be safe. Everyone there, from Bo Bottomly to some poor, lost, drug-addicted kid, has lost it one time or another, one place or another. No salt poured into wounds; just compassion, love, understand-ing, sympathy, and practical help. We all have our common needs of grace. Grace—that provides *forgiveness,* which nullifies the stains and claims of the past; and *power*—to live Christ's life in the world now and in the future.

Mike and Karla Yaconelli helped mold this atmosphere of loving trust and compassion among the people at Grace Community Church in Yreka. It is still in good hands. And yes, finishing Marilyn's proposal went quite smoothly…with a little help and hilarity.

Just recently, Marilyn led communion, something she very seldom does. There were some first-time visitors. There were two labeled goblets, one with wine and the other with juice, and a loaf of fresh-baked bread from Elaine, one of our group, who also signs for the deaf.

Marilyn said, "We invite any and all of you to join us in this communion with our Lord. This is all about what Jesus did for us and to remember what He has done for us. It doesn't depend upon how good you are or what you have done. My heavens, look at the disciples when they were at the supper with the Lord; they still had all kinds of hangups when Jesus served them…but it is all about remembering Him. So we'll start at the back and everyone come. Ted, will you play something on the guitar?"

Reflection

Mellowing comes with age. There is not less determination, but more discernment in approach, more discretion in actions, more reflection in evaluation. God's grace, gentleness, and patience have not been wasted on the Sewards. They are moldable clay; noble and plain vessels, available for the Master's use.

> *"As we pass through life, certain experiences crystallize into special precious gems that sparkle in our memory."*
> Marilyn Seward

Chapter Fifteen

Into All The World

She knows the hills of Lebanon, the heat of the Moroccan sand,
The beauty of old England, the plains of Kazakhstan;
She travels as an ambassador, not just a tourist's fare,
But for the King of Kings, Who has business everywhere.

Bruce and Denise had been missionaries with Frontiers in Kazakhstan. Denise was a local gal from Scott Valley and a former student of Wendell's. Their field had experienced some serious challenges and Frontiers organized a conference for the whole Central Asia Region (CAR) to be held in Cha Um, Thailand. They wanted someone to handle a program for the kids who came with their parents so all the families could get acquainted. Bruce and Denise thought of Marilyn. They knew she'd taught school for over thirty-five years, and had organized several school and church-based children's programs.

When the call came, Marilyn quickly responded. Joined by local friend and recent widow Jeanette, and others recruited by Frontiers, they converged on Cha Um in January of 1998. Marilyn had responsibility for the curriculum—right down her alley! She soon had everything under control. The children ranged from infants through high-school age. Marilyn's experience included all ages of students, so she was in her element.

Marilyn gives us a glimpse of the action on this first of many trips. "As it turns out there were six of us to work with about thirty kids. We didn't have the best of facilities so we quickly improvised. This meant using the roof of the conference hotel for recreation and various other activities. We did a story-based curriculum tailored to the different age groups, the kids learned songs, we did crafts, and everyone gathered on the roof for fun and games. All in all it was a great time. I had the opportunity to meet many missionaries, and to encourage several of them. Mostly they just needed to be hugged. I thoroughly enjoyed myself, and am certainly willing to do it again. I have a lot of respect for these missionaries, some of whom are living and working in very trying situations."

In recent years Marilyn has taken several teams to minister at conferences to MK's (missionary kids), whose attending parents live and minister among Muslims. She goes willingly, paying all her own expenses, and often helping others on the teams she recruits. Oswald Chambers says the obedient Christian must "...transact the business of their lives along the line of the heavenly vision, no matter the cost." The remainder of this chapter provides anecdotal testimony of Marilyn's "transacting of business."

Marilyn has been involved in sixteen missions conferences in various countries of Europe and Asia. Her first experience was in 1998. Frontiers, an organization "serving, respecting, and loving Muslims... in the name of Jesus," gathers their field workers together periodically for mutual encouragement, sharing, and planning. Beginning back in the seventies, they have considerable staff in Arabic-speaking countries and cultures. Most of the regional or international conferences run about five days, and whole families attend. This means there are kids, dozens or hundreds, that need to have something to do. They come with a built-in excitement and expectation of just being with their peers from around the region, many of whom they have never seen, and others not since the prior year's conference.

Marilyn's desire is to make this a very special and meaningful time for them, and she has. Rather than have parents care for their kids and miss the sessions, arrangements are made for others to provide the care. *Care* is an operative word here, but it just begins to tell the story. Tailor-made programs are provided for each age group. But the story is broader than just the conference. Preparing for, and getting to and from the conferences produce their own unique experiences and often disclose some personal attribute of the traveler.

✝ ✝ ✝

"Oh my, one time we had to carry all this equipment. We were in the airport in Frankfurt trying to get down to the train level. Each of us carried a suitcase and a carry-on. Marilyn is leading the pack with some other large duffel bags. The locals tell us to put all our stuff on top of the carts and take them down the escalator. So here we go. Marilyn gets in front so all the carts are behind her, and we're all behind them. Then the whole thing collapsed—just tipped over on Marilyn. All the carts and luggage come crashing down on top of her and her dress gets stuck in the escalator. She's being pulled into the escalator and these bags and things are scattering everywhere. We're running down trying to tear her dress loose with all this equipment on top of her. She just gives a big jerk and gets her dress loose, jumps up, brushes herself off, starts piling bags on carts.

"Everybody else is standing there stunned. Astonished. She is in her seventies and we're all younger… some much younger. I couldn't believe it. I asked, 'Oh, Marilyn, are you OK?' I know she had to be hurting. She really didn't say anything, we just got loaded up and off we went. She never mentioned it again. A couple of days later when I went over to her room and caught her in her nightclothes, she had bruises all over her arms and legs. She never even reacts to it, ever! She just takes all that kind of stuff in stride." Marilyn's close friend, Pam, who has accompanied Marilyn on other trips, told this story.

In 2000, Marilyn was asked to play a vital role in a blockbuster meeting, Frontiers' International Conference, held at Kent University in historically significant Canterbury, England. Canterbury, a cathedral city in East Kent in South East England, is the seat of the Archbishop of Canterbury, head of the Church of England and of the worldwide Anglican Communion. The challenge was to assemble a team and materials for about one hundred ninety kids. She recruited some friends; Joan (Jo-Ann) from Etna, a talented woman with a servant's heart, amazing creative ability, and an avid quilter; Gloria, also from Scott Valley, another capable servant-hearted person with a missionary heart; and very close friend, Pam, from Bonny Doon in the Santa Cruz Mountain area of California. Gloria and Pam are businesswomen. All have interfaced with Marilyn before in some capacity. Several other helpers were recruited by Frontiers from a variety of venues.

It seems Marilyn had problems with the chosen topic, *spiritual warfare*, for the lower ages, and petitioned the powers that be to allow her to pick something she felt more appropriate. Upon approval she scrambled to get more appropriate materials. She wanted *Castle Fair*, which was about serving the King. The setting is medieval England with a castle and Roman ruins. It was a perfect match for their setting and she knew the kids would just love it. She also arranged a field trip for about one hundred kids to Canterbury Cathedral, just down the hill. When the day came, they all trekked down the hill and ate lunch on the cathedral grounds.

"We went to the Roman ruins and museum and the kids could see the old tiles that had been laid over fifteen hundred years ago. I shared with them the situational story about Augustine from Kent, telling how he came to England in AD 597 and began to Christianize that whole area starting right there in Canterbury. The older kids were awestruck, and the younger ones seemed spellbound."

Marilyn is a pro when it comes to story-telling, and has a unique skill in presenting the spiritual lessons—to any age group, for that matter.

A highlight of the conference was the honoring of Greg Livingstone, founder and long-time leader of Frontiers, for his vision and leadership. He founded the mission eighteen years prior in 1982 on the campus of the US Center for World Mission in Pasadena, California. (We were then both on the USCWM board of directors). During the ceremony, Greg would pass the baton to Rick Love, US Director at the time. Marilyn had a hint of excitement in her voice as she shares about the day. I made sure the recorder was on.

"Joan cooked up this idea of a quilt, a huge queen-size quilt. The kids traced their hands on individual cloth blocks and wrote their names. Then they helped sew it all together and Joan finished it up that week. The children also practiced some music during the week. A children's pastor from Mesa, Arizona, did a wonderful job of putting together the musical program. We had a staff of about forty including thirteen teenagers from a Presbyterian church in Michigan. They were absolutely wonderful.

"We had the widest variety of people. Those attending the conference were from the whole world, all eight of Frontier's regions. Everyone seemed to have the sense this was something really special. All these missionaries and their families held in common a love for the

Muslims they wanted to reach, and they had a fraternal love for one another. On top of that, add this special honoring-time for Greg Livingstone and you just knew the Holy Spirit was up to something. You could feel it in the air.

"When the last evening arrived there were about nine hundred adults in the audience and close to two hundred kids all arranged to sing. The last song had to do with the story of Philip who went out in the desert. The chorus asks, 'Who will go, who will tell them, who will give them the Gospel of peace?' And then 'I will go, I will tell them, I will give them the Gospel of peace.' They sang that for the parents, and by the time the kids got to the second or third verse, all nine hundred parents were standing, raising their hands, shouting, praising the Lord, crying their eyes out. It was just an amazing experience!

"The next day was the final day; everyone was preparing to leave. In the morning you could look down this gorgeous green carpeted slope to the Canterbury Cathedral, coming up out of the mist. Parents with kids were gathering around the book table we had set up. I brought books for every single child, all by ages, so they could pick out a book. One hundred ninety of them. They had painted some white tee shirts and those were all lying out on an embankment, so everybody could go by and find their child's shirt. Gloria was doing the hand bells with the kids. And those bells, ringing out across the land…there was something enchanting about that whole thing…

"Next was the Pinewood Derby with about one hundred-fifty kids participating. The men of the two families from Idaho, the Grays and Tuckers, cut out the derby car bodies before leaving the states. Bringing them and all the other parts for the little cars, they had the kids paint and assemble them during the week. They had bought the lumber for the track at a local lumber yard and on this last Sunday, 'Derby Day,' everything was ready to go. It was a truly gala affair! Run by age groups, with kids and cars everywhere, and oodles of parents standing by to watch their kids' cars, excitement ran high. The early afternoon was filled with hoots and hollers and semi-organized pandemonium. Not a soon-forgotten day for young or old, I assure you.

"Then the last thing was the big Olympic circle. Pam brought an Olympic torch which was placed in the center and then eight streams went out, one for each region. Every one had a little Olympic flag and some Olympic memorabilia. Pam thought to bring all this stuff and it was exactly what the occasion required. All the parents were there to watch. These last two days were so special. The kids were into the real meaning of it all. They had sung the night before, 'We will go,' and now they were marching outward carrying the Olympic flag, like they were really going to go into all the world. And you know, I feel many of them will. Their parents are such noble examples. What a privilege it was to be there, and to be involved in some small way."

I don't know about you, but I really get blessed reviewing this account. I'm utterly amazed at what took place. Eternity alone will reveal the results, all the tributaries that flowed forth from that place through all those lives. There was a tremendous amount of pre-planning and preparation, plus purchasing supplies they took: dozens of bags, hundreds of pounds. The message and impact were special and what a memorable time this was for the kids…and the parents. And to top that—Marilyn takes a picture of each child; has those who can, write a note to their grandparents—on both sides—then when she gets home develops the film, writes another note to the grandparents, and sends it all out. Time and commitment and compassion! I've read some of the responses from the grandparents to Marilyn and they are utterly appreciative.

Yes, Marilyn is definitely a world-class missionary! And God was faithful to the vision He gave her those many years ago. He used her earlier training, her experience, her gifts, her abilities, her struggles, her compassion and acceptance …her obedience to the vision He gave her, and her desire to serve to accomplish the purpose for which He called and sent her. *He is faithful and He will do it.* His hand is on top of our hands on the tiller. He is the Master Navigator. He furnishes all that is needed for the journey.

The sixteen conferences Marilyn organized teams for have been in eight countries: Thailand, Kazakhstan, England, Germany, Morocco, Lebanon, Jordan, and Croatia/Slovenia. A typical and touching anecdote relates to the 2004 conference in Croatia. Before leaving, it was standard procedure for Marilyn to send a form to all the parents requesting, among other things, that they put in anything about their children they thought would help make this time special for them. One mother's statement caught Marilyn's attention. "Anthony has trouble in groups of people and he has trouble adjusting, so just kind of let him go. Don't force him into anything because it will upset him." Hmmm...

Marilyn shares, "He was nine years old and sure enough, he didn't want to sing, he didn't want to stand up, he didn't want to do this or that. So we just kind of let it go. I told the kids later in the week there would be some books and videos they could choose from to take home. I had them out on a table and Anthony saw the video, 'Brother Bear.' He had seen this advertised and really wanted it. Videos are not available where his family is living. So he asked, 'Can I have that video?' I said, 'OK, I'll make a deal with you. If you will do the bells and if you will do the puppets with the kids, I promise you can have that video. But there's only one.' So he practiced with us.

"When we did the program the puppets were first. The kids had to kneel down behind a table covered with a black sheet and perform with the puppets on the table top, so the parents couldn't actually see their kids as they manipulated the puppets making them dance and sing. It was a great time, and I looked over at Anthony and there was just pure joy on his face. It's too bad his parents couldn't see that, and he did his part really well. Then all the kids lined up and played the hand-bells. And Anthony was right out in front ringing his bells on cue, one in each hand, smiling. I looked back in the audience and you should have seen his parent's faces and the tears. This was the first time he had ever participated. It was very special. He is one kid in Croatia that I will miss seeing."

Times like this with the Anthonys make it all worthwhile. Seeing some measure of positive transformation in a person is what ministry is all about. It adds a special reward in answer to the question, "Do you care enough to go?" It's really back to the basics, isn't it? Marilyn's caring love and acceptance applied with wisdom in this situation helped one little boy enter into a new world. That's missions at its best. The number of times this occurred in those sixteen conferences where she and the others helped, only eternity can reveal. Wise love is powerful for changing lives.

She has Great Commission vision, has the whole wide world in view,

She's an active mobilizer, and a strategizer too;
She wants to see each believer, involved in a meaningful way,
Sharing in Christ's mission, whether they go or stay.

Marilyn's last trip with Frontiers was in June of 2006. Two days after returning from a conference in Jordan on the Dead Sea (my wife Judi went along to care for the babies, and also David, a local Forest Service employee who worked with the older children), Marilyn headed off to Thailand for a Central Asia Regional Conference. She had recruited a team of four from the valley, including Karla and her fourteen-year-old daughter, Melissa, and Melissa's friend.

Gloria, now a frequent traveler with Marilyn, relates an interesting story. "I'm experienced now so I thought I should go along and help Marilyn. I figured she'd be beat with such a short turn-around plus handling all those seventy-pound bags. *Sure, I'll be her helper!* Well, I got good and sick early in the conference and I was sick all the way home. Marilyn said to me, 'Don't fret about a thing, we'll handle it, you just go to bed.' They handled it. When I got in line at the Bangkok airport, who was standing in front of me? Marilyn! She grabbed my luggage, handled the counter people, and got me where I needed to go for processing and then she bought me tea.

"Then in San Francisco, Karla got sick and Marilyn had to mother both of us. We still had our flight to Medford to go. She says, 'You girls just sit down.' She went hiking and found Pepto-Bismol. I thought, *how humiliating.* I made my whole plan so I could help Marilyn. She literally got us all home. We would have been a mess without her. She's beyond human!"

The conferences Marilyn helped with were much more than opportunities for the missionaries to get more input. They were "share, care, and prayer" situations; where they could also understand and bear one another's burdens; where the kids could relate to others and develop lasting friendships; where everyone could celebrate together, understand one another, and love one another—Body life.

These are the ones who have responded to, "Who will go?" with "Here am I, send me." Marilyn and Wendell echoed that response early in their lives, and as these accounts illustrate, God moves in mysterious ways His wonders to perform. It is not always the best that go to *Jerusalem, Judea, Samaria and the uttermost parts of the world*, but it *is* the willing and obedient. And in that obedience, they become the best.

Yes, Marilyn played a vital role in making this experience meaningful and lasting. Combining her experience and skills with her compassion for children, and underwriting these with the understanding that eternal consequences were in view, God was able to mold something special in those young lives that is beyond comprehension on this side of eternity.

Reflection

We humanoids calculate too much, while faith watches from the sidelines. A commitment to a vision, coupled with availability, obedience, care and compassion, has produced a positive result in multiplied hundreds of lives…of all ages. Marilyn counted the cost of obedience early on and is spending it all for the nations … as did the One whom she follows.

> *"It is not necessarily at home that we best encounter our true selves. The domestic setting keeps us tethered to the person we are in ordinary life, who may not be who we essentially are."*
> Alain de Botton, *The Art of Travel*

Chapter Sixteen

Biased Toward Love

*"Consistently, He spoke the truth against a sea of opposition.
Shockingly, He lived fully in His personal life exactly what
He preached in public.
Time after time, He stood heroically alone for what was right,
regardless of what it might cost Him.*
Bruce Marciano[1]

Wendell Seward is seemingly a simple man. That is, he doesn't put on airs. He wouldn't be classed as an intellectual. He has few hobbies. Likes to read, watches his alma maters' football, and sometimes basketball; is friendly and cordial to almost everyone. Pastored churches for fifty years. He taught school for thirty-five, and was continually involved in the community. He comes across as meek and mild-mannered...and as quite hospitable. The reader should gain a balanced view toward understanding the keynote of his life. No man more truly loves from the depths of his heart, and is more loyal to Jesus Christ. But the very intensity of his love, and his desire to reflect Christ, exposes him to much injustice and accusations of short-sightedness. He has his faults, but lacking in loving acceptance is not one.

So, providing a faithful portrait requires giving an account of his several roles. To think of Wendell as merely a pastor, or to consider him solely through the lens of his thirty-five years of teaching in the public schools, or primarily as a public servant, would be to lose the sense of proportion. Even the symbiotic functioning of the combination would still have a sense of sterility if not attended by his loving care, compassion, and concern.

---

1   Bruce Marciano, *In The Footsteps of Jesus (Eugene, Harvest House, 1997)*

What specifically renders Wendell one of the most admired persons in the area? Why and how has he impacted the hundreds, perhaps thousands, of lives that he has? Why has he held over 800 weddings? Why is he called the *Shepherd of the Valley*? What is it about this kind, mild-mannered man that makes his life so remarkable—so powerful? When I read Marciano's *In the Footsteps of Jesus*, the thought going through my mind *was*, "Vintage Wendell." When I read about warm and caring, wise and spirit-filled Father Tim in Jan Karon's *Mitford Series*, I see Wendell.

A mainline theme in Wendell's Christology is the maxim, "*Every person has intrinsic value.*" He has an "acceptance" theology. And, like Jesus, when he encounters unclean spirits, alcoholics or druggies, sickness and/or disease, sinners of all stripes and other "enemies," he is not afraid of being infected by their sin or sickness, but "infects" them with Jesus' compassion, understanding, care, love, truth, power and grace.

Not long after leaving Scott Valley Berean Church, the Sewards heard from the community that the church leaders had not allowed Job's Daughters (a youth arm of the Masons) to make their annual presentation of singing "Onward Christian Soldiers" in the church meeting. Wendell particularly was deeply grieved. Rejecting the very people who should be exposed to Christ's love and acceptance was unthought-of during their years in leadership there. What were people afraid of—contamination? Were they threatened? Did they think these young girls were going to contaminate the church, the congregation, Jesus? What was their rationale? Were they afraid of what other churches might think? Did they think they would send the wrong signal?

"We know there are always those among us," Wendell observes, "who are still struggling with these kinds of issues and fears, but to reject people is in a way condemning them. That's the *natural* way and maybe the *safe* way, but it certainly is not Jesus' way. We need to approach them with a different spirit; a spirit of love and acceptance."

When love is conditional, the enemy of man's soul is quick to use the *condition* for his own purposes.

"It's amazing," Wendell relates, "how much we learned in our early Christian lives and church-going that we had to unlearn later on. And that's tough to do. The truth can set you free, unless it's laid on you like a law -- something you do rather than something you are, because it's something the Bible says we should do, or you think it says we should do, instead of really coming out of a heart of love for people and for the Lord. We try to behave because we think we should rather than because we are being transformed by the Spirit of the living God. One of the most difficult and life-giving experiences I've had is to change from living under legalism to living under grace. Mike Yaconelli and Mark Hatfield really helped me here.

"Seems like most evangelical churches…maybe most churches… are caught up with 'teach-teach-teach' without 'be-be be.' If we're not modeling Christ in our lives, then our teaching is hollow…hypocritical. We're just puffing up ourselves and those who hear us. If we'd only had Jesus' words without His life, our lives would have a whole different meaning and purpose. He lived His words. His life taught us the truth. His words confirmed it."

Certainly Jesus' life and words, and the Sewards' living examples of the same, greatly influenced and even transformed the well-meaning ministry of their friends, the Opfers.

Gary and Kathy Opfer and their three children arrived in Scott Valley in the late Eighties. Gary had been a high school band leader and teacher in San Diego, California. They both were interested in becoming actively involved in missions. They joined the LIGHT International staff for a time, then made their way to Europe where Gary taught music and band at the Black Forest Academy in Southern Germany. They then gravitated to Croatia, where they worked with refugees, and finally settled in Kosovo where they started a school and were involved in a range of humanitarian efforts.

"When Kathy and I arrived in Scott Valley (1988), we brought a lot of baggage with us—negative, destructive, unproductive, 'Christian' baggage—and we were not even aware of the load we carried! Our church background was fundamental, traditional, evangelical. We were always careful to dot all of our "I's" and cross all of our "T's." We lived by the letter of the law versus the spirit of the law. We were critical, accusatory, judgmental, finger-pointing 'saints' …but then we met Wendell and Marilyn Seward.

"We witnessed for the first time a genuine Christ-likeness we had never seen before…and it didn't take long. They opened our eyes and revealed to us, not by preaching to us, but in action, that true faith in Christ is indeed demonstrated by loving God and loving others. Jesus made this truth abundantly clear in word and action throughout His earthly ministry. So, how did we miss it? I think we emphasized doctrinal truth and left our first love. (Rev 2:4)

"What we experienced through the lifestyle and ministry of Wendell and Marilyn was a paradigm shift in our own personal lives and in the lives of our family. Their examples of love, grace, humility, acceptance, compassion, forgiveness, and generosity changed our lives forever! After being introduced to the global needs of humanity through the influence of Bob Waymire, we spent the last decade ministering to Albanian Muslims in war-torn Kosovo.

"Compelled by the lessons learned through Wendell and Marilyn and by the grace of God, we were able to more fully give ourselves to others in need. We were taught to think of others more highly than ourselves, to look out for the interests of others,[2] to give without expecting anything in return,[3] to love God with all our heart, soul, mind and strength, to love our neighbors as ourselves.[4]

"What had the Sewards imparted to us? The very reality of a loving Father, for love is of God and God is love. (1 Jn 4:7, 8, 16) And "those who love God must also love one another." (1 Jn 4:21) This is who Wendell and Marilyn are and this is their legacy to us. We are forever grateful!"

I'm reminded of some words Oswald Chamber shares in *My Utmost For His Highest* that I think are apropos here: "Through every cloud (trial) He brings, He wants us to unlearn something. God doesn't want to teach us in our trials so much as He wants us to unlearn some things—His purpose in the cloud is to simplify our belief until our relationship with Him is exactly that of a child—God and my own soul..."[5]

Time is one commodity available to everyone, and Wendell uses it mainly for investing in people's lives. His hospital visits are legend-

---

2   (Phil 2:3, 4),
3   (Lk 6:35)
4   (Mk 12:30, 31)
5   *My Utmost For His Highest*, July 29th

ary. He is a familiar sight to most nurses, doctors and receptionists in the Yreka and Medford hospitals. Dozens and dozens of times he's driven the hour and a half to Medford, Oregon, to see people who are hospitalized.

When our teenage neighbor, Joey, was in the Shriner Burn Center (severely burned in a power-line incident) in Sacramento, Wendell drove the ten-hour round trip three times to spend some time with him and take his aching mother to lunch. Joey didn't attend the church regularly, nor did Wendell know him well. But this wasn't important. Joey's mother, Karla, an ardent believer, admires Wendell's love and sacrifice.

"To me, Wendell is a wonderful model of how a true Christian should order his or her life. And you know, he was going through a rough emotional struggle at the time as they were leaving the church, but he never mentioned it once. It's never about him, it's always about others. I've known Wendell for several years and he is always the same. He is the one person who loved me no matter what. I told Jesus I really wanted to be like that."

Karla shares another testimony crowded with significance. "My daughter, Melissa (14) and her friend, Amber and I joined Marilyn in 2006 as part of her 'children's care team' at the Central Asia Rally held in Thailand. This was the first time my daughter and I had traveled overseas. It was an amazing trip with many memories, but of all the experiences of that trip, the one I know these young girls will remember the rest of their lives, and so will I, is returning home. As we were walking off the plane into the terminal there was Wendell, dressed in a suit and holding red roses.

"Wow! This is how he receives his bride Marilyn when she returns from her trips. Clean shaven and handsome at 80! Melissa, Amber and I after 30 hours of travel, loaded our bags into the Suburban and we headed home quite worn out. But not too worn out to discuss this phenomenal behavior - those young girls were really touched by what Wendell did. I am a single mom, and I worry at times for my daughter's lack of a father figure; how will she know what a truly Godly man will look like, and in that moment I was so thankful to Wendell for always showing up! He was showing those girls how Jesus would treat his bride and he didn't say a word. He was just…just Wendell. At fourteen the two girls witnessed the real deal.

"The church goes to great lengths and expense to capture the attention of teenagers and I watched an old guy who's been married sixty years do it by the way he treated his wife. That is remarkable character."

Humbly and openly, He marched across cultural barriers, decrying centuries of racist arrogance. Never a respecter of persons, unconcerned with status, wealth, gender or popularity, He stood champion and friend of the "little guy."
Bruce Marciano[6]

Wendell's broad realm of acceptance includes those of other faiths. As previously mentioned, he and Marilyn helped perpetuate a monthly potluck attended by a variety of church leaders and others. Catholic, Adventists, Greek Orthodox, Pentecostal, Protestant, and other Christian ministry individuals all participated in this monthly time of food, fellowship, and prayer. This gathering epitomizes Wendell's inclusive approach to life.

Invite everyone and let the dissenters exclude themselves. Don't alienate those whom God loves. Don't be intimidated by those who say we send the wrong signals when we hobnob with others who do not believe exactly as we do, or with the miscreants and "heavy sinners"… that we are condoning their ways. This certainly isn't Jesus' position. Jesus reaches out to all of society saying "whosoever will come" and "I love you so much I went to the cross for you"… "I didn't come to condemn you but to save you from yourself and for Myself."

Wendell has the remarkable trait that continues to help and not condemn a person when he or she fails again and again. It seems to Wendell every time is the first time—he doesn't seem to get discouraged. He knows what is in man, but more he knows God's love is not limited, defeated, damaged, or discouraged by man's repeated failures.

A case in point is Donny, who has lived with the Sewards off and on for the past three years. They've helped him in several ways: car, bank account, job, etc. Donny falls from time to time, but the Sewards

---

are always there to help. Over time, Donny has been gaining the victory and is now living a fairly stable life.

One fairly common observation voiced by people knowing the Sewards is, "Although their personalities and giftings are quite different, yet they seem to get along well, and as a couple they've ministered to thousands of people." I asked Wendell one day if he would share about some of the adjustments he had to make in his relationship with Marilyn.

"Well, Marilyn had just graduated from a very conservative Bible college when I got out of service. She suggested we go on a picnic. It was an awkward thing for me. I felt more at home watching the ballgame going on in the next park than I did in the picnic area where I was expected to interact with church people. I guess it was some kind of reverse culture shock. I didn't realize it at the time, but I had gotten so hard when I was overseas. When I'd see a buddy on a stretcher trying to hold his intestines in, I just had to harden myself and go on. It's a very hard thing to overcome and I didn't want to talk about any of it. Marilyn told me later that some of those early days were pretty trying and sometimes scary to her.

"Then, of course, look at the positions the church assigns to men: He's the head of the house, he's the one who's supposed to be 'in charge.' I discovered later on that some translations and interpretations of scripture compound this problem. Of course, Marilyn had gifts of leadership and I did not, so, consequently, we were struggling for territory. I was frustrated because she knew how to do things that I felt I should do. I would come up with some suggestions that sounded pretty good to me and I could tell by her attitude they were pretty childish. I think mostly it's a growth thing. Sometimes, though, the way she said things seemed like a put-down.

"One time I was at Mt. Hermon for a pastors' conference and the speaker said, 'Just talk among yourselves, then after you are all acquainted, each of you share one thing about your family home life you would like to change. When all have shared, then pray for the person on your left.' There were seven at each table. Well, on my right was a big black pastor from Fairfield, and boy, he knew exactly what I was going through. He really prayed. I felt so good. He prayed that I wouldn't see my wife as a mamma whenever she tried to give me instruction. And I let it go for quite a while.

"Then one day while driving back from Medford something came up. We were just coming down the mountain into California and she subtly criticized something I'd said and told me the way it should be. I stepped on the gas because I knew that always got her. She said, 'Wendell!' And I said, 'I thought that was over with.' And she said, 'What are you talking about?' And I told her when she talked like that it was always in the back of my mind that she was like my mom giving me instructions. And just being able to confess that to her, that day I traded a mamma for a wife. About that same time I thought, *Lord, I'm supposed to be submissive to her, we're supposed to be submissive to each other. So I'm just going to back off.* As soon as I took the pressure off, it started a brand new relationship. We started enjoying each other at a deeper level.

"There never was a time when we would have ever traded mates. I always knew that I needed her just for her inspiration. She sensed she was really supposed to marry me, even though neither one of us knew anything about love. She wasn't too sure she loved me, but she always thought God wanted her to marry me. I was afraid to ask God because I knew I wanted her. So looking back, I feel I really didn't have to ask; he told me."

Without hesitation, He went out of His way to care for the most objectionable people of society, never turning a hungry soul away, always taking time to love an unlovable or care for an uncareable, knowing He would suffer ridicule and rejection for it.
Bruce Marciano[7]

One time at breakfast, Wendell shared the following interesting story. He had just returned from performing a unique marriage in Yreka. "I received a call a week ago from some woman in Eugene, Oregon, asking if I would perform a wedding for her twenty-year-old daughter who is pregnant and has diabetes. The girl's fiancé is fighting in Iraq and it would be a *proxy*[8] marriage. Someone else would stand in for the

---

7   Bruce Marciano, *In The Footsteps of Jesus*
8   The State of California makes provision for proxy marriages when one person is in the service and deployed overseas.

groom. Before I could say much she told me this is legal in California, but not in Oregon. They had contacted the county offices in Yreka, and someone gave them my name.

"She explained the baby was due the first of September, but because of the diabetes this could change, and they wanted to have the marriage take place before the baby was born. The husband was on assignment in the Baghdad area, and they were trying to get him home before the baby arrived. This seemed iffy, so to play it safe they wanted to have the wedding now. I was caught off guard for a moment, but then told her, 'Yes, I would be glad to do it.' She seemed very relieved, and we went ahead and set up the arrangements.

"Well, yesterday the wedding took place, and I thought it was very meaningful, and the family and witnesses also seemed to think so. I know I can come under a lot of criticism, but who am I to decide what they should do and not do, and whether or not it is appropriate. I don't really feel like she is in sin…but I don't know. I'm leaving that up to God. It is man that made our marriage rules anyway.[9] I felt it was important to let her know someone cares and to let her know whatever actions they've taken doesn't separate them from God's love. She may suffer some criticism and possible rejection (I hope not), so I think it's important she knows she is a valuable person in God's eyes. I hope she gets some positive reinforcement to help her through this experience. It would be a real blessing if her husband could make it home before the baby is born. I was really impressed by the mom. This girl is fortunate to have her standing with her." As has been previously stated, *"It isn't about condoning, it's all about redeeming."*

Reflection

Wise is the person who invests in the lives of others; who sees the potential of people, not through fleshly eyes. Who sees in each soul intrinsic value. Who, when nurtured with loving acceptance and a genuine yearning to understand, will blossom and give forth the sweet aroma of a grateful life.

---

9   Wendell said later "the story of Isaac and Rebekah in Genesis (ch.24) came to mind where she rode a camel into Isaac's camp and jumped off and she and Isaac went into the tent and 'consummated the marriage.' I suppose many people will have trouble with this, partly because of social and cultural traditions, and partly because of the way they see this in scripture. I was thinking if I didn't do it she would feel rejected and that would do more damage to her than if I did. She probably already had condemned herself, and I'm sure Satan was reinforcing that. Love and acceptance needed a chance."

Chapter Seventeen

Tickings

"There is power in servanthood that transcends all notions
of power sought after so avidly by the world."
Senator Mark Hatfield[1]

One way of expressing what makes Wendell tick is to look at some of his quotes, and quotes of others recorded over the past few years. The following are from spoken or written messages:

"We don't need tickled ears, we need broken hearts that are bleeding for others."

"Don't take a day off to attend a religious festival. Your employer will have to have someone take your place. Think of him or her first, not your job or your paycheck."

"It's only after I take away the rules and obligations, then what I am acting out of is the real me and it should manifest the life of Jesus."

"There's no wall so thick or so high it can't be broken down by the power of God's love."

"Some mistake freedom for disorganization."

"If we don't accept them, who will?"

"A Great Commitment to the Great Commandment and the Great Commission will grow a Great Church."

"When we focus upon the sin, we can't see grace."

"Nobody needs to be told they are wrong. The Holy Spirit has the job of convicting of sin."

"Anyone can see a fault and tear a person down. It takes a real person to see that which is good and then strengthen those traits. We need to learn to 'accentuate the positive.'"

---

1   Mark Hatfield, *Between a Rock and a Hard Place*

"A life centered in the love of Christ and His compassion leads to a well ordered, disciplined life…and not the other way around."

"Should I reject someone just because I don't agree with them? I'm sure Jesus never agreed to a lot of stuff I did…and stuff I still do, for that matter."

"When others write you off, Jesus writes you in."

"If I look at his shortcomings instead of his soul, I'm no real help to him."

Some observant quotes regarding Wendell from others are also revealing:

"Without good people like you to serve as spiritual anchors to the community, we would be lacking much indeed. I have great respect for you and your family and look forward to our interaction." In a letter from J. Kirk Andrus, Siskiyou County District Attorney, Yreka, California

"He may not have the fanciest sermons. But I don't care, love outweighs it all. And that's what comes across." Francyne, Etna

"Are you Mr. Seward?" " Yes." "Well, you talked to my mom when she was going to have an abortion, and I'm sure glad you did, because I really am glad to be living. I really enjoy life, and I just want to thank you." Young girl on the Jackson Street School playground in Yreka who heard the man standing near was Wendell Seward.

"Well, he's really strong on not ruining a listening ear." Jerry, Etna

"I was giving my opinion against somebody and he (Wendell) could tell I was getting right on the edge of condemnation and he says, 'Now wait a minute, do you really want to condemn that person?' and then I realized what I'd done. Habit…bad habit." S. Higgs, Shasta River

"Wendell's messages are so good they nearly always make me cry because it reaches my heart in a special way. He's no theologian, but he's deep. Deeper than most people realize." Janette, Etna

"…this pastor said something about there only being 'three evangelical churches in the valley.' I wish he wouldn't have said that. Saying those kinds of things separate. Wendell would have never said that." Ibid

"I've always remembered a message Wendell shared in which he said, 'When they are training people to spot counterfeit money they don't have them study the counterfeit bills, they spend their time studying real money.' He was telling us not to focus on the activity in the evil realm but to spend our energy studying the real thing, that being Jesus. If you know him real well, anything counterfeit will be obvious." Karla, Old Etna

"Respect and admiration for the Sewards are domiciled in a thousand hearts." Bo B.

"Their service toward others so consumes their lives they don't have time to worry about their own troubled experiences." Author

"You know, after living with you for fifty-eight years, I think your top priority is meeting people's needs. You have a soft heart, a mercy thing that seems more important to you than almost anything else. We've had a few arguments about that." Marilyn Seward, 2004

"Wendell looks for and finds the good in every person." Ken Medema, 1998

"With Wendell it isn't difficult to separate the wheat from the chaff." Mike Yaconelli

"He speaks from the heart more than from the mind." Wanda, Etna

"Wendell has grace 'til the cows come home." Pete, KCOC

"Over eight hundred weddings and four hundred funerals?! Goodness, goodness, goodness…my, my, my! Can you imagine how many people were exposed to God's view of marriage and love through Wendell in all that? It's gotta be a big number. And to think how many families were comforted at those funerals. My, my, my." Matt; Bouse, Arizona

A long-time alcoholic woman was in the hospital and Wendell visited her a few times. Once, after he prayed, he leaned down and kissed her forehead. Several years later, fully recovered, the lady told Wendell, "You know, the turning point was the day you kissed me on the forehead. Somehow it just gave me strength and hope to go on. It seemed someone really cared."

"This is a church for people who don't like church." Guillermo, from Spain, (August 2007) at Grace Community Church in Yreka

"I'm enjoying my time (with the Sewards); so much love. There is just so much love. I hope Heaven will be like this." Guillermo, to the author, August 2007

✝ ✝ ✝

Guillermo Bruño's testimony to the Sewards is included here to illustrate how the process and prowess of the Holy Spirit works on a continuing basis in lives that have been exposed to the power of Jesus' love, grace, and acceptance. Guillermo was an exchange student from Spain, living with the Sewards during the school year of 1985-'86.

He was just seventeen when he arrived. He has kept in contact with the Sewards, and after receiving a teaching credential, Marilyn helped him get a job in Happy Camp, California, in 1997. He returned from Spain to teach that one year, then went back to Spain where he taught English in a public school. Wendell and Marilyn were his "second parents." The last time he was in Etna was in the early fall of 2007, before Wendell discovered his cancer problems.

During the two months of Wendell's illness, Guillermo called every week, and talked to Wendell the day before his home-going. Three and a half months after Wendell's "exodus," Marilyn received the following precious message from Guillermo.

"I didn't understand very well why God put so much effort in order to make me one of His sons. I honestly don't have the feeling of having done much to find Him. I rather feel I did completely the opposite. It's as if He had been knocking, knocking, and knocking at the door of my heart for almost eleven years, and I pretended that I couldn't hear anything at all. It was only when I found myself in the most desperate position that I began to respond to Him. I think before then I was a dead man walking.

"I don't know what the real Hell is like, all I know is that I've been through some kind of hell in this life of mine, always tormented by my past, my present, and the future. It was then when I realized that nobody, absolutely no one under the face of the earth was going to be able to help my tormented body, soul, and spirit, to get rid of my addiction and all the other sins it had led me to: lying compulsively, manipulating other people's feelings, stealing money from my folks...and I had no sense of guilt at all. I had never done any of these things before; well, I guess I must have lied many times in my life, but not that way.

"All I know now is it was as if the Enemy had taken complete control of my existence. I cannot put the whole blame on him; I must admit that I also played my part to let all these things happen. It was only when I couldn't see the end of the tunnel that I gave my heart to Jesus. I decided to let Him in and do with me as He pleased. It was utter desperation; I could picture myself ending up in jail, because of gambling debts—or in an asylum, because I had become mentally unbalanced—or dead; some people decide to put an end to this miserable kind of life by committing suicide.

"I wish I knew the exact date, or at least recall the exact moment when all these thoughts, all these worries vanished, but it was something progressive; it took its time. When it was ripe enough, it was as if that burden had been taken all of a sudden from my shoulders. Many defects have completely disappeared: I can't swear anymore. I try to be tolerant, in the sense that I don't despise (in my thoughts) those who don't share my points of view, especially religious views.

"I'm more talkative. I'm learning how precious it is to see reality through other people's eyes, not only believers. I'm realizing how distorted my vision of reality has been, and I'm not referring only to that period of my life with my gambling addiction. I make an effort to show my affection for others, including my folks, my colleagues, my beloved students...and I receive this affection in return, which is something I don't recall to have felt, except with you, Wendell, the Waymires, and other people in Etna. Once I thought that God only existed in your little, precious town and the rest of the world was hell. Fortunately that's not the case at all. Ha-ha!

"Above all, what I can share with you is that I have this 'hunger' to keep on growing in the Lord and walk the whole rest of my life with Him. I do know what it is to walk this journey we call life, without His love and without His presence in your heart. Not having Him in my life is something I just can't picture; I think I'd die—not only spiritually, but perhaps in the physical sense too. He has saved me in all dimensions.

"Last Thursday I found a couple lines from Isaiah 65:1. The verse says: 'I revealed myself to those who did not ask for me; I was found by those who did not seek me.' I was literally astonished, believe me; it was quite a revelation to me, and perfectly explains why it was Him who found me and not the other way around.

"Marilyn, I wish I could express either in human or angelic language what you and Wendell did for me. Sometimes I wonder whether I would have met the Lord if it hadn't been through your example. The thing is, when I was with both of you for the second time, back in 1997, I started to wonder why your lives were so full of blessings and joy. I hadn't seen anything like it in my whole life; I had never experienced such an atmosphere of peace before. Of course I've seen you both sometimes going through difficulties and tribulation just like everybody else, but there was *something* there that you guys had. I wanted to learn what it truly was and have for myself too. I felt curious to find out. And it wasn't the scripture or the church so much as it was above all your living testimony that led me to Christ. You helped me to understand where the scripture says, 'the greatest of these is love.'"

Reflection

Frequently, profound expressions of gratitude come (sometimes many years later) from the lips of those whose lives have been transformed by the loving influence of another person. More often than not, the influential person is unaware of the full impact they are having on the one whose life is in the process of being transformed …which is as it should be, because it means the "influencer" is acting out of purity of heart, expecting nothing – not even gratitude – in return. It is in this way -- through sincere and selfless love for one another-- that God's revolutionary, redeeming work is accomplished in the world.

"His (Jesus) life taught us the truth; His words confirm it."

Chapter Eighteen

Servant Leader

---

*"Healing love must drop all personal choices and preferences,
all fastidiousness, all desire to get something out of our union
with Christ; and be willing to work for nothing, be a faithful
servant, not a pet."*
Evelyn Underhill[1]

Mike Yaconelli[2], now enjoying his Lord face-to-face, shared the following at Marilyn's seventy-fifth birthday celebration. It was a great evening attended by dozens of friends from near and far.

"I thought it would be a great place to begin by asking the question, 'What would it have been like in Biblical times if Marilyn Seward were there?'

The Good Samaritan: She would have beaten up the robbers, taken the money back, brought the injured man to her house, started a home for injured robbers, written a grant for roadside security, and run for city council to have the road rerouted.

The woman caught in adultery: Marilyn would have picked up a rock and stoned the stoners, taken the woman into her home and let her live there for a year, created a "women caught in adultery" center, made Wendell preach a series on the sin of adultery, and petitioned the Roman government to begin a rock removal program.

If Marilyn had been at the feeding of the 5000, she would have heated the bread, cooked the fish, organized the disciples to serve the food, and told Jesus to 'take five' until everyone had eaten.

---

1   From: *The Soul's Delight*, from <u>Selected book by Evelyn Underhill</u>, Keith Beasley-Topliffe, editor (Nashville, Upper Room Books, 1998) pp. 50-51.
2   Mike Yaconelli went to be with his Lord October 30, 2003. He authored several books including, *Dangerous Wonder* and *Messy Spirituality*. He led or co-led Youth Specialties for thirty four years, an organization that trains and equips youth workers.

If Marilyn had been in the boat with the disciples when Jesus showed up on the shore after he was resurrected, she would have kicked the disciples out of the boat and told them to go to Jesus, she would have chided Peter for taking his clothes off, rowed the boat in herself, filleted the fish, served fish and chips to the disciples, and with the rest of the one hundred fifty-three fish she would have organized a meals-on-wheels program for those who didn't have enough food.

If Marilyn and Wendell had been Adam and Eve, the first time Wendell started looking amorous, Marilyn would have smacked him on the head and said, "Here, have an apple, don't go getting any ideas. We're not going to sit around naked all day—we've got work to do."

Seriously, if there were one Bible character I could compare Marilyn Seward with, it would be Paul. Marilyn is like Paul with a skirt, traipsing around the kingdom of God, breaking new ground; passionate about truth; committed to the kingdom; missionary heart; no nonsense; take-no-prisoners attitude; no time to waste. Marilyn can be wrong, she can be stubborn, she can be blunt and direct and like a bull in a china closet. She can also be firm and forceful and insightful and informative...and even tender and caring.

I could talk all night about the driven, active, worker bee that is Marilyn Seward. Oh, the achievements, oh, the accomplishments, oh, the projects, start ups, stacks of work she has done. Oh, the people whose lives she has touched. Oh, the work she has done for the kingdom of God.

But I want to talk about Marilyn Seward, the person. And I can tell you that is not what Marilyn wants me to do. Marilyn doesn't like talking about herself, nor does she want anyone else talking about her. She is uncomfortable revealing the person who is Marilyn Seward. There's a term for it. It's called "humility." Marilyn, you are a woman with a vision and a purpose, and with the warm and loving heart that is required to increase the bounty in the Kingdom with good fruit that remains. You are a woman of compassion and legendary hospitality. Your capacity to demonstrate love in the practical and spiritual realm is an awesome thing.

"You truly are, Marilyn, the woman spoken of in Proverbs 31."

✝ ✝ ✝

One way to obtain a description of some dimensions of Marilyn is to listen to the words of those who have had relationships with her, and/or been impacted by her life.

Pam is a businesswoman living with her husband Dave in the beautiful redwoods near Santa Cruz, California. Through their relationship with the Sewards their lives were turned around. Pam has traveled on overseas trips with Marilyn, and they are confidantes. She shares the following:

"David and I wanted to get married, and I knew very little about it, so Marilyn said I needed to go with her one weekend. We went up to her old church in Colton (Oregon) to some sort of reunion. There was this big thing about her and I realized I didn't really know her. You know how you form an image of someone, but obviously this is based upon whatever relationship you have, and ours hadn't been all that personal or intimate. While we were there she took baths instead of showers. She didn't blow-dry her hair…had never owned a hair dryer! She and Wendell are not like old people who don't know about showers and hair dryers. They are current, they know all about those things. When you go to their place they don't have any fancy furniture or stuff like that, but you don't notice those things because the hospitality is so warm and genuine.

"And oh, she eats pie! I hadn't had pie for ten years, no pie—it isn't healthy, with all that Crisco. But she was just so simple and beautiful. I just fell in love with her that weekend, an amazing weekend for me, amazing. We had fun, we really did; I mean, I was myself. From that point on there was nothing I wouldn't say straight out to Marilyn, no matter what it was. I would tell her anything, even things you ordinarily wouldn't want to say to anyone.

"Last year when we were in Germany, we stayed at Kristin's apartment in Frankfurt. Kristin had stayed with the Sewards in the States, and they were very close. They helped when she was going through college. Kristin was planning on getting married. I have a visual of Marilyn and Kristin sitting on the bed together, with Kristin's head on Marilyn's chest and they're talking about sex! I was blown away.

"I thought, *what a relationship they have*. Kristin is hardly thirty and Marilyn is seventy-five. Most people don't get to know Marilyn like this. They see the energetic, no-holds-barred woman who is famous for getting things done. But she's such a girl too. She's soft and tender and she cares about little girly things. She would tell me stories…you know…in many ways she's just a girl. But she doesn't appear that way. She's not a girl when you first meet her. She's a schoolteacher or a principal or a mayor."

"How do I describe Marilyn? I can't." This astute observation was made by beautiful, brown-eyed Mania from Venezuela, a student who spent her 1993-'94 school year in the Seward's home. She is now a top salesperson with Burlington Carpets in Caracas. Yes, to most, Marilyn is an enigma—puzzling, to say the least. However, Mania did go on to portray Marilyn in a way that evokes the response, "Yes, that's her!"

"You see" Mania muses, "Marilyn is like a bright and shining star, full of energy. She can guide you when things are dark. She's always there and wants to help you. She is very comforting and helpful. At first she teach me every word because my English was no too good. She was very kind and told me very patiently everything. If you have doubts about something, she just talks to you and she guides you very sweet. When you look at her you know she is thinking, thinking. She does so many things and she just needs to think. So many people come to talk to her about so many things. She is just full of hospitality. She just has to manage so many things and then take care of her family and all of us. It's hard to describe. Sometimes we talk about the Lord. She loves so much the Lord. When I got my first letter about my coming she spoke about the Lord, and I knew it will all be OK."

Kristin from Germany once lived with the Sewards and she stays in touch on a regular basis. Her beauty and warmth are attractive, soothing to everyone she meets. She and Marilyn have had a very close relationship since 1992. She is now married to Michael, a Lufthansa pilot and they have a chubby little son, Janik.

"Marilyn is strong willed, but loving and caring, and enthusiastic about everything she does. When she does something, it's 150 percent. She's a workaholic. I have found out over the years she is fun. And she's very sensitive, especially when it involves people that she cares for. Anything about God gets her so excited. Her faith is so alive. She's very set in the ways of the Lord. I think that gives her the power that she has. I think she just goes in the love of God. Otherwise, I cannot imagine anybody having that energy, especially now leading all those children's ministries for the missionary conferences all over the world. Oh, my goodness!

"If Marilyn has a weak point it is that it's very hard for her to accept the love that she is always giving to others. She doesn't seem emotional or very touching like Wendell, although she has become more touching in the last three or four years. She always just wants to solve problems. She wants to get right down to the point and work on it. She doesn't take the time to relax because she doesn't want anything for herself. She doesn't want to get spoiled. I always wanted to give her massages, but it's like she doesn't need much touch. She just wants to go, go, go. I think that's a weak point, not to be able to sit down and rest and let other people take care of some things, and just really show her they love her, and do it in an emotional way."

Pam (a different one) taught with Marilyn for several years in the small, rural Quartz Valley School. She says Marilyn is the one who tutored her. When Marilyn retired, Pam took over as principal.

"Nothing stops her from reaching out to people. That was one of the things she did for the families at the school. One Christmas I said, 'Marilyn, what could I do for a family?' Marilyn is always doing something, so, like a little girl, I wanted to do something for this one family. I sew…I'd love to make a Christmas dress for a family in need. So she says, 'What would really be nice is if you would invite them to your house for Christmas Eve.' We always had a big Christmas Eve party for the kids with Santa Claus and everything. And just like that she says, 'It would really be nice if you would invite them.' I couldn't believe it. But I did! And it was the right thing to do. That's what she's always doing… reaching out. Giving your time is a precious gift.

"There was no mediocrity…there was no halfway…there was no compromise. We will present the best program, we will do the best, and we will provide the best. And she had the best staff working for her. I learned what I know in this teaching and administration area from her. You somehow try to make every kid feel like they can produce the best and they do, they're fantastic.

"Marilyn and Wendell, through the many exchange students they've hosted over the years, have affected a lot of people including, of course, the students themselves. Marilyn says, 'Pam, we need to have someone keep this student just until their host family is ready, probably a week.'

"I say, 'Marilyn we'd have to move our bed into the other room and give the girls the bigger bedroom,'

'Well, what's wrong with that?'

"I say, 'That would be inconvenient.'

'Well, what's wrong with that…it would be good for you.'

'*Stay a week.*' Ha-ha! We fell in love with her and she stayed a year."

> *She's still involved in teaching, on call to cook at the camp,*
> *She's traded in her candles, bought an energizer lamp;*
> *She still runs to and fro, using her spiritual gifts,*
> *Such that Father, Son, and Holy Spirit, have to work in shifts.*

Not long ago, during Judi's and my weekly breakfast with the Sewards at Bob's Ranch House, Marilyn was looking a little tired and haggard. She lamented, "I can't understand this feeling. I don't want to go to church. I'm just not energized to go to church. I just don't want to do anything, and I've got lots to do."

I thought my hearing-aids were playing tricks again. But then I understood. She was just being honest. She was tired. Grace Community Church is a very warm and joyful group, full of fun and freedom, with lots of sharing, and the Sewards draw great energy from there. So what we were really hearing was that the Energizer Bunny's batteries were finally beginning to flag a little. She was tired already(and she was only in her late seventies!).

This reminded me of a remark her son, David, made referring to his mother and all she does. "It's tough to be in charge. In about everything she's involved in, she's in charge, or close to it. That's tiring, sapping. But, it is one of those situations where you know you can do it, so you do it. I knew when she got on the city council that mayor was soon coming. Both of us suffer fools very little, you know. I have this drive that says if we're going to do something, let's do it, get it done and quit messing around with all the other nonsense. I know that's from her, because that's absolutely how she is."

David's second wife, Joann, shared that one time she was missing her own parents who were both deceased, and she just needed to talk to someone. "I really didn't feel I knew her all that well, but really wanted to talk to her. So I picked up the phone and called Mom (Marilyn). She was so warm and so loving. She gave me just what I needed. The feeling that I had when I heard her voice; she is so calming and loving, and I thought…this is so neat. I had wondered if I would ever be able to have that kind of relationship with David's mother. But the Lord is so gracious. I am very fortunate to have people like my in-laws in my life. I love them so. They are precious, precious people."

> *There's no doubt in our Valley, she's the "woman of the hour,"*
> *Who can help you plan a wedding, or host a baby shower;*
> *To serve the town as mayor, she just manufactures time,*
> *She'll whip up a grant proposal that will meet the bottom line.*

Beth and her husband, Jack, live locally near Etna. Beth taught in one of the local schools. The Sewards were involved in her daughter's wedding and her mother's memorial service. She says this about Marilyn:

"When I first met Marilyn, I just knew there was no frivolousness here. I really appreciated that. I met her on a professional basis as a teacher. I could see that she was not one to mince words. You needed to be very honest with her. I felt that's what she was giving: honesty. That's why I have always felt so privileged to lean on her when there was need for direction; she would see through all the peripherals and get to the core of it. And so I knew if I needed a straight answer I could rely on her. I also learned she had a tender heart and sweet spirit. She is so easy to be around. I'm sure that's Jesus in her."

> *Scott Valley Berean Church and the Quartz Valley Unified School,*
> *Salvation Army, the Library, and the Etna swimming pool;*

Teen Edge, the Theatre Guild, and Youth for Understanding,
The "Citizen of the Year!"—we can call that outstanding

A lady called Martha came to the door one day when the Sewards were having company. Marilyn states, "Somebody told her she should meet us because she was on a spiritual quest. So I invited her to come back and we had dinner together. When we were alone she said, 'I really appreciate your inviting me for dinner, but I want to be open with you. I'm a lesbian.' I told her, 'I already figured that out and you probably know we don't think that's right. But I do not want that to affect our relationship. I like the way you think. You're a thinker. You've got a head on your shoulders. Your quest is honest. So I don't want that to affect our relationship." Vintage Marilyn.

Reflection

Influence that is exercised in producing positive and lasting results comes from serving rather than commanding. From servant leadership rather than command authority. A humble servant does not mean a weak servant. But rather one totally available for the Master's use. Humility is a bed where wisdom lies. For the casual observer, Marilyn's humility and wisdom and adoration of Jesus are sometimes overshadowed by her energy, abilities and desire to serve Jesus. Yet both are totally involved. She's a Mary-Martha combination of loving devotion and practical faith.

You're always made to feel at home, in this safe haven of rest;
Warm and loving hospitality, cooking at its best;
She snaps her fingers deftly, a casserole appears;
Loving arms to enfold you, a shoulder for the tears.

Chapter Nineteen

Lessons from Wendell

"Picture Him storming in against overwhelming opposition,
giving his literal all–his very life–to rescue the helpless,
the widowed, the orphaned, the crushed, the rejected,
and the despised. I don't know about you,
but in my book, that's the living definition
of "hero" – the true definition of hero."
Bruce Marciano[1]

Judi and I were talking with friends Don and Diana recently, and they were telling us an anecdote that took place just prior to their getting married. Diana is a home-grown girl (one of the Can-Can girls) and had lost her first husband. Wendell had a part in her coming to Christ. Don had been in the valley since 1997 after a somewhat checkered career. He also had been previously married. Don, a big, easy-to-be-around guy, tells this story:

"Before we were married, Diana and I were co-habiting. We figured, by golly, we were sixty and we could make our own decision on that one. Well, it was pretty easy to tell what was going on, I guess, because my car was often parked in Diana's driveway or out front … and it was still there in the morning. Invariably, Marilyn, in her pink duster, was out on her walk before I was off to work just about the time Diana and I were sitting in the front window having breakfast. And we would look up and say, 'Well, there goes Marilyn.' And we talked a bit about the fact that we weren't married yet and how this might be affecting people."

Then Diana added, "One evening, Marilyn was gone on one of her trips so we invited Wendell down for dinner. He walked in and started

---

1   Bruce Marciano, *In The Footsteps of Jesus*, (Eugene, Harvest House, 1997)

tearing all the cushions right off the sofa! He threw them on the floor and was standing there. And I thought, *What on earth! Gosh, what is happening to Wendell!?* Then he starts feeling all around the sofa and in the cracks; then he said, 'Just what I thought. Don told me he's been sleeping on the sofa. If he had, there would be change in here.'

"I could have died, I was so embarrassed. He picked up the cushions and put them back. We had a good laugh…but I was still red-faced. Then one evening after being out, we came home to find a note on the door. It was from Wendell and it read, 'Willing to do very inexpensive weddings on a moment's notice.'

"Well, as you know, we finally took him up on it. And Marilyn must have changed routes because after that we hardly ever saw that pink duster go by."

"It all boils down to whether or not people feel accepted." Wendell is speaking. "Jesus told us to love our neighbor, and made sure there wouldn't be any mistake about who our neighbors are. He modeled unconditional love…well, that's who He was. He was sensitive to everyone… who they were and how they felt. Everyone wants to be loved. That's where we must begin.

"It's unavoidable. Especially when we remember that the Word of God is not some black and white pages. The Word of God is a person. When we try to separate the written word from the living Word, we've lost the whole message. So anytime I open up that Bible if He's not in it in a personal way, then it's just literature. And I think that is what it ends up being a lot of times: A lot of teaching, but no real life. When the teaching is laid down as a formula or a 'to do' list, it can be reduced to a set of laws.

"Paul says, 'The law kills, but the Spirit gives life.' (2 Corinthians 3:6) Christianity is a person, not a set of creeds. And…that person is love. If God's Spirit is present, there is love and life. When you think of Jesus saying, 'I came to seek and to save the lost;'[2] and, 'He that is whole doesn't need a doctor, but those who are sick'[3], you realize His whole message was about people.

---

2   Luke 19:10
3   Mark 2:15-17

"It's so interesting how we human beings, and even animals, know when we are loved and how we respond to it. Love is such a powerful attraction. It's pretty simple when you get down to it. It's simple…but not always easy."

He goes on, "It reminds me of what Mike [Yaconelli] wrote in one of his books about a seminary student who felt as though he wanted to do some calling and decided he would go to the high-rises. In the first apartment building, he knocked on the door and a woman answered, a cigarette hanging out of her mouth, a screaming naked child in the background. She said, 'Whatever you have to say, I don't want to hear it,' and shut the door.

Not really knowing why he did it, he broke two very profound rules. He went to a store and bought a pack of cigarettes, a big bag of diapers, and some groceries. Returning to the apartment he said, "I want to help you take care of the child." He even had a cigarette with her. Now, "good Christians" don't smoke; "good Christians" have no business going to a single mom's apartment. He said after an hour and a half when things had calmed down and they were having a good talk, it was then he realized what true ministry is: Showing people you care…then they can believe God cares.

"People don't care how much you know until they know how much you care. And if your heart is pure, as this young man's was, it doesn't get too wounded by the criticism of others."

Wendell tells the story, "After we got acquainted, a guy named Larry who used to live here, wanted me to go with him to Mendocino north of San Francisco. When we arrived, his lawyer friend invited us to a potluck dinner. It was certainly not like one of our potlucks here. The corn was only about half-done and things like that. And the girls, when they wanted to nurse their babies, just nursed them right there and they weren't careful about what was seen or not seen. It was rather interesting.

"But I did learn something from Larry. Their language wasn't the best, and Larry said, 'When you folks say, "Praise the Lord" and "the Lord told me this," well, if you get offended at our language, that's what your language sounds like to us. It sounds so horribly offensive: "The Lord told me." In other words, you've got it in with a higher power; and we don't.'

"Well, I'd never thought of that. I didn't realize what our God-talk many times does to the world. And we're supposed to have the ministry of *reconciliation!* It's our job to be careful not to offend them, even if they offend us. That's the reason I'm enjoying reading *Blue Like Jazz*[4] where they set up their confessional booth in Reed College. The fellows were asking forgiveness from the other students for misrepresenting Christ. It's scary how often we Christians present a repellent caricature instead of the winsomeness of the real Jesus."

Dave was a tree-feller in our valley when he first met Wendell. He had an alcohol and drug problem and Wendell had taken an interest in him. He was also going with a young business woman in the valley, Pam, who would later become his wife. Dave tells of a pivotal incident in his life.

"Wendell took me up to see Bo Bottomly. I guess I'd had enough conversations with Wendell that he felt he wasn't able to be direct enough with me in the area of my problem, so he took me up to Bo's. Bo is quite direct. In not-too-nice language he told me that I was just full of it. That was good for me. But Wendell seemed taken aback. 'What's wrong with him?'

"When we returned to the car he said, 'I don't know what got into Bo, I'm not sure coming here was a good idea. He was rather antagonistic toward you. Are you okay?'

"And I said, 'You know what? He was probably right.'

"Wendell was all on my side. When he took me there he probably wanted Bo to say something like that but wasn't expecting him to be so strong. But I know now it was just what I needed. It helped me make the decision to say that I would go to a treatment center if I did it again. Wendell had a big part in getting my life turned around."

Wendell's life is considered remarkable by most who know him…even at a superficial level. His warmth, friendliness, and humor make him easy to be with. Yet the principles of the life he lives are neither totally understood nor practiced by very many. Even so, the fruits of his ac-

---

4   *Blue Like Jazz*, Donald Miller (Nashville, Thomas Nelson Publishers, 2003)

tions are recognized in him, particularly by those who have come under his influence.

Here's an example: It is March of 2006. Wendell and I are sitting in their living-room and Marilyn is out and about. Our discussion turns toward meeting people where they are. The recorder is running:

"I'm not very strong on just teaching the Bible to those who I meet for the first time. Lots of people we want to reach feel more comfortable in the tavern than they do here in our home, or especially in church. We want them to know we care. God sends us to all people, and he doesn't tell us about those we're not supposed to go to. I figure first we need to establish some kind of relationship, then take it from there. Most everyone has real needs and wants to know there's help somewhere. We can't expect them to feel comfortable in our church culture.

"Some of our men's meetings were held at the tavern on Sunday mornings to get away from any religious atmosphere. We always wanted them to tell it like it was, and not act religious. We had a former Oregon football star, Paulson, who played for the New York Jets, share one Saturday. Bill Coe, who had a ranch in Quartz Valley, got real excited about his message. Bill was interested in football and sports, and Paulson gave him a New Testament. We invited the mayor, who was a Rams fan. He always came but didn't claim any relationship with Christ."

Wendell, always one wanting to be culturally relevant, in this case regarding the ranchers in attendance, shared this homey parable: "You know if all we do is gather together and talk about the life we should be living, we're like a warm and stinky manure pile. It's only when we are scattered around in the field that we do any good." He does have a point.

"Even in the church we tried to change the culture from the normal church atmosphere. One time when the Can-Can girls told me they were going to be performing in a parade in Callahan, I asked them if they would come to church that Sunday and do one of their dance routines. We'd been meeting with them in one of their homes.

"Well, they didn't all want to at first, only five of them came...but they didn't have their outfits on and I was a little disappointed. Well, just before they went on the stage they took off their outer clothes and they had their outfits on underneath. They were really a hit...and although I'm sure it shocked some of the more conservative people, the word got around that the Berean church was the place to go for 'special entertainment.'

"Too often we look at what people do and that turns us off. I try awfully hard not to let that happen. God has put eternity in each heart, and sometimes only love and acceptance can get to that. People can tell whether you really care or not."

Reflection

Yes, people can tell whether or not you really care. Wendell's non-religious and caring nature made the ground level in establishing relationships. He wasn't one to stand in the well-worn footsteps of tradition. He pretty much let others set the scene, responding with amazing adaptability without compromising his beliefs and convictions. He wasn't one to take center stage. He was quite willing to let the Master write the script. As a result, many had their lives turned around and became solid and productive citizens.

> *"It has nothing to do with condoning,*
> *it has everything to do with redeeming."*
> Mike Yaconelli

Wendell from time to time was asked to write short articles for two local newspapers, both having wide circulation in the county. He had been a member and president of the Ministerial Association, and was the pastor with longest tenure in the area. He also had fairly high visibility as the result of his many involvements in community and county organizations and affairs. People for the most part admired him...and would listen to what he had to say. The following is from an article published in the Siskiyou Daily News titled, *Union is not always Unity.*

"One of the fond memories of my youth was the once-a-month Farmers' Union meeting. I hung out with the big boys and witnessed their antics. One special incident that sticks in my mind was when the boys found two cats lying peacefully beside the barn. They caught them and tied their tails together and hung the cats over a clothesline. I was horrified at the cruelty, but the boys thought it great sport. Those poor cats, who were friends, were clawing, screeching and scratching until they finally worked themselves free of each other and fell full force to the ground. They ran in opposite directions, and I don't remember seeing them again that summer.

"The boys facilitated union, but there wasn't any unity. Talking of "one great Church union" has a similar ring. Nearness does not bring unity. Even if it did, what a bland tune it would play. We all have different functions and act differently, but we are to operate in harmony with one another. If we could learn to enjoy the differences and not see them as threats, real unity would be more easily achieved.

"In our Scott Valley ministerial get-together, five of the pastors were chatting after the meeting. The Seventh Day Adventist pastor mentioned he was going to preach on the Holy Spirit. The Pentecostal pastor then asked each of us what we taught concerning the Holy Spirit. After the Catholic, Seventh Day Adventist, Methodist, Berean, and Pentecostal pastors gave their views of this cardinal doctrine, we were amazed at how little we truly differed in essentials.

"The power of Christ's love is the power to lift a person above the defeats of this world. The negative and judgmental treatment some people receive is similar to witchcraft. I know this is strong language, but it is the same thing practiced by some occult groups to negatively affect someone they don't like. If anyone says, '*I love God*, yet hates his brother, he is a liar. For anyone who does not love his brother, whom he has seen, cannot love God whom he has not seen.'[5] *When others write us off…Jesus writes us in.*"

Reflection

An unknown person said, "I'd rather see a sermon than hear one any day. I'd rather one walk with me than merely show the way…" For those "in Christ" there is an *undeniable reality* in a person who walks the walk rather than just talks the talk. There is an *unforgettable fragrance* that follows along their way. There is an *unquenchable optimism* about their persona. Their life is one of *unimpeachable integrity* and *unvarying success* (although perhaps not by the world's standards). Wendell fills this bill.

---

5   1 John 4:20

Chapter Twenty

Lady Marilyn

Marilyn sees below the surface, where the feelings often hide,
She discerns the wounded spirit, the things one holds inside;
She applies the Balm of Gilead, when she finds the wound is deep,
She hurts with those who are hurting, and weeps with those who weep.

The few hairs stringing down her cheeks made a fitting frame for her soft blue eyes. Taking off her green gardening gloves and waving them at a passing neighbor, she let out a deep sigh and said, "Good timing. I'm ready for a break. Just a second, I'll get us a cold drink."

Waiting under the shady apple trees, I considered this seventy-eight-year-old matriarch with deep appreciation. The incredulity of the thirty-three years we had known each other passed the curb of my brain, and I realized I was sitting on holy ground...I could sense the presence of God.

How misleading that moment could be to those seeing only a few facets of this woman. After all these years of weekly breakfasts, I wondered if I really knew her. Judi and I have been many places and had many experiences with Marilyn and Wendell, and I think one of the reasons we are still so amazed comes from how we've seen them keep life so simple and to the basics. Basic love and kindness, gracious acceptance, servant spirit, warm hospitality, insightful wisdom, generosity, joy and freedom...all of these things that seem so hard for most of us to grasp and be and do...they just seem to do without any fanfare, fuss or muss. I think this is the authentic Christian life. Why is it when someone lives it, we think they are super-saints? Take Mother Teresa for instance. She is and does what Jesus asks us all to be and do, and is highly acclaimed. Yet, it is just the "normal Christian life." Well, normal to a few...like the Sewards, who have the discipline of self-sacrifice uppermost in their lives. Lives lived in obedience and self-sacrifice develop traits of wisdom and humility.

Seated and sipping lemonade, I asked Marilyn what her hobbies were.

"Let me see...I guess you could call it 'hobbies'; I enjoy gardening, reading and cooking. One of my frustrations now is I'm so busy I don't get to spend the time I would like in the yard paying attention to the garden. I remember when I was five or six, my mother gave me a little plot for a flower garden, and I loved that. It got into my blood. In high school I did some drama and enjoyed that. Oh, I used to love to *sew*, but I don't do that much anymore. For other things, I love to teach and I like public speaking. I love to sing. I used to sing quite a bit, and led some choirs. Music is important. I love studying and going to school.

"I enjoy *hospitality*, having people in our home. We love cooking and having people over for dinner and out here in the yard. The fellowship is meaningful and important. We loved having our kids, our exchange students. That's fading out now; it's the end of an era. Wendell is eighty and I'm not that far behind. But we still enjoy having people over, especially in the summer when we can all be outside under these trees. We've had lots of out-of-town friends come by. We really enjoy hosting them, and having friends over to meet with them.

"Over the years we've enjoyed having people living here, although at times it has been a real challenge. Many of them came for healing, and we were glad to help, but it also presented some problems, especially when two or three people were here at the same time from different cultures and all. But it all turns out great because most of the people are quality people who just need some care at a particular time, and we are able to help.

(I think everybody is a "quality person" to the Sewards.)

"Most of those who lived here have gone on to successful lives. We hear regularly from some of the students decades later. It's great to have that relationship."

You never know what God might have in mind...one of those challenges came to live with the Sewards: Axel, from The Netherlands.

"Axel came to us in late August of 1979 to be one of our short-term exchange students. With Axel it was really 'short term' because he stayed only about four months instead of nine. He didn't like rules and refused to obey them. He didn't want to go to church or Sunday School, which was in our home. He also insisted on driving a car, which foreign exchange students are not allowed to do. He became so rebellious we had to find another place for him…he wanted to go to a city…so Youth for Understanding, the sponsoring organization, arranged for him to stay in San Francisco.

"You could have knocked us over with a feather when ten years later, Axel called Wendell and wanted to know if he could come for a visit. Of course Wendell told him we'd be happy to have him…although I was wondering how things might work out. It turned out he *really missed the loving atmosphere*' he had previously scorned. When he arrived, he enjoyed talking with us and was very interested in spiritual matters. I remember he made the comment one day that Wendell was still wearing the same coat as he was when Axel was there ten years earlier. In early 1992 he brought his father, saying he wanted him to experience some of the warmth he felt here. Periodically, over the years, he would call and it was obvious God really had a hold of his life.

"Thanksgiving Day, 1992, we received a call from a hospital in San Francisco. Axel was waiting to leave the next day for Hawaii, when the pain in his head hit, reminding him of a similar pain two years earlier when he was operated on for an aneurysm. He called 9-1-1, asking for assistance. An ambulance arrived and took him to a local hospital. When the hospital called me they said he was pronounced dead. They had called Axel's parents in Holland, and they gave the hospital my name and number. I jumped in my car and headed for San Francisco, talking to his parents first and helping make their flight arrangements.

"Well, I got to the airport in time to meet Kitty and Jan. It was quite an emotional moment."

Kitty recalls, "We were so surprised to hear someone call our names…'*Yoo-hoo, Kitty and Jan…over here.*' She was so wonderful; she took us to a hotel and made all the arrangements for us. She also helped with the arrangement to take Axel's body back to Holland and even got a refund of Axel's ticket to Hawaii, which we used to help with our expenses going home. I really don't know what we would have done without her help! She drove us to Etna where the church put on a wonderful memorial service for Axel. It was so special. How could they do this all in such a short time? We are so grateful for the love that Wendell and Marilyn have shown us. We know that Axel found peace

with God and so did we. God took such good care of us through the
heart and hands of Wendell and Marilyn."

Reflection

Being loved and accepted when you know you don't deserve it makes
an indelible impression on the heart, breeding hope. Love changes
things—and lives!

Marilyn continues: "Ever since I was a little girl, the cry of my heart
has been to *please God* -- whatever that means, and whatever it takes.
I was little when I became a Christian and I longed to be spiritual. I
didn't know the phrase, 'God's person' or anything like that. All I knew
was I wanted to be spiritual. I wanted to be godly. And that always
had to do with people, obviously. We had to make a lot of choices. I
particularly had to learn lessons about interruptions in my plans…that
interruptions were part of God's M.O.. I needed to learn to plan the day
but then be willing to have that plan knocked out of kilter.

"I enjoy *missions*. It's part of my DNA. I feel strongly God wants us
involved in some meaningful way in the reason he came to earth: to
seek and save the lost. We've had an interesting history in this regard.
The vision for missions came while I was a high-schooler at Maranatha
Bible Camp in Nebraska. We didn't get to go overseas, so we've ended
up extending hospitality to missionaries, having them here to church
to speak, and supporting them.

"In 1998 I started working with Frontiers and their conferences.
Those were such meaningful times, and it really helped me understand
the real challenges a lot of missionaries face. So at the age of seventy I
finally got to be a *foreign* missionary. Of course, Dick Hillis, founder
of Overseas Crusades says, 'you are either a missionary or a mission
field,' so in that way we are all missionaries.

"I've always loved *teaching*. All during the thirty-five years I was
teaching in the public schools, I was also teaching in the church,
sometimes both children and adults. I find the Bible fascinating and
love to teach its truths and then watch that truth, and love, change
people.

"Wendell and I have taught in many different situations and cir-cumstances. We've taught individuals, and small groups of Christians and non-Christians. We've taught many Bible classes -- many of them not in church. I feel teaching is such a privilege and need. Also there are a lot of good books out there with good truths for how to live a meaningful life in today's world. Then comes the challenge: putting the truths, as you say, "into shoe leather."

"I am goal-oriented. Wendell ... not so much. I want something set up so I can see 'this is where I'm headed, and this is why I'm go-ing.' I've found myself in all kinds of administrative and organizational leadership situations, usually because if I believe in something, I will volunteer to become involved. I seem to have gifts in some needed areas. Also, I find many public groups are so wound up in bureaucracy and paperwork, it is difficult to get the job done. I try to help bring more harmony and civility to the table.

"I've wanted to be *light,* but also *salt* in society. I remember one lesson about the treasure we have in jars of clay. Salt and light are two of the treasures we carry, and they need to be shared. One of the stories was about Elijah, who took a jar of salt and poured it into the water that was bitter and it was never again bitter. It was purifying. We Christians should be making positive moral and ethical impacts…we should be helping to *purify* society. And of course salt also brings flavor. And like you have said, *salt only works in touch.* I like that perspective as it brings more meaning to Wendell's and my ministry of being in touch with so many people, whether they come to our home or we meet them where they are.

"And then in teaching we are sharing the light, the truth. Light ex-poses those things that work against us, and we can see them for what they are. Of course, Jesus is light, so when we're talking about light we are talking about His truth and illumination. Wendell and I think that the name of your organization, LIGHT International, is right on; wanting to bring the task into the light so everyone in the world is visible to those who are trying to reach them. I'm glad Wendell is on your board."

The following comment by Marilyn gives insight into her humility and compassion for "making disciples," and the fact she and Wendell were never *self*-satisfied.

"There is one area where we could have done better. I think I've become aware in recent years, and it makes me a little bit sad, that we didn't go about transferring what we knew and did very well. I think we could have done a better job of teaching other people to do that. I wish we could have done more about raising up another generation that would be more loving and accepting. I know people have told me the last few years that I often did too much and didn't involve enough people because I was so driven. That is sad in a way. I wish I had done better in this area."

With all they accomplished there was no pride, but a sense that they could have done much better. This provides us keen insight into their basic motivation.

"In the last few years I've grown clumsy. It's hard *getting old*. I've fallen several times, had some bad bruises and black eyes. I had my arm in a sling with a bad shoulder from a fall. I had a whole bunch of baggage fall on me on an escalator in Frankfurt, and was lucky to get out of that as well as I did. I was so embarrassed. Then I've fallen on the ice and banged my head. All in all though, I have never been what you would call real sick. One time I lost all my energy for about three weeks. That was really unusual."

Marilyn's activities are not merely "to-ing and fro-ing"—they are result-producing. While others are still thinking about it, Marilyn's doing it. This causes her no end of criticism and problems.

Looking back, it may have been that Marilyn's fast pace and busy-ness were part of the problem in bringing some separation between her and daughter MeriJean. There were many things they did together, especially in the home, but there were also many things that Marilyn may have thought were going on in MeriJean's mind that were not.

For instance, the move to Etna really was a serious point of contention for MeriJean. However, she was struggling with some relational things with her mom before that, some relating to legalistic issues such as her clothing "code," and "approved" activities that embarrassed her with her friends.

Marilyn knew the move was causing some discomfort and stress, but she considered this normal. She wasn't aware of how deep the hurt and resentment were until they festered into serious rebellion. It seems Marilyn knew something was amiss, but felt, "Oh, she'll get over it."

MeriJean did not get over it. Even before the move to Etna there was a need for communication that didn't occur.

MeriJean experienced some of the same problems and frustrations with her own daughter, Leora, who more or less followed in her mother's footsteps in this area of teenage rebellion. When Leora was fifteen, she went to stay with her grandparents (the Sewards) for most of her high school years.

Marilyn says of that time, "MeriJean was in a struggling place, and we were glad to take Leora in. We soon found she had some of her mother's rebellious streak. Life became quite interesting, that's for sure. We were very concerned about her relationship with a boy she was spending a lot of time with, but any mention of this triggered her anger. She would respond with something like, 'It's my life, and I can live it the way I want.' She did…and trouble seemed to compound. This sounded very familiar."

In those days Marilyn and Wendell were often arriving home late from teaching. There were others living in their home, and some were students arriving home the same time as Leora, so there was some interaction and relations built with peers. Leora talked some with Wendell, but when asked normal questions by Marilyn about her personal life, plans and whereabouts, her replies held a tone of resentment and in this way was similar to her mother at the same age. It seemed evident that some generational trait-transfer had taken place between her MeriJean and Leora.

It is painful to see young people in this frame of mind. Each one has such potential and much to offer others, but this gets totally sidetracked when they become protective of relationships they themselves later admit are unhealthy. But at the time, they are so emotionally involved, it seems to blind them to being objective or rational, and so they explode when confronted—especially if they already have a chip on their shoulder.

Leora continued to spiral downward over the years, eventually getting into very serious trouble and facing manslaughter charges. After being diagnosed as bipolar, she was interned in a rehabilitation facility and is showing remarkable progress. Her story is still being written. In the meantime, MeriJean and Leora have developed a precious, God-honoring relationship with each other, and with Wendell and Marilyn. Our Redeemer lives!

Reflection

All kinds of unimaginable secrets hide behind the shield of silence. It is not uncommon for these to join company with vain imaginations and false suppositions. Penetrate this silence from the wrong premise or understanding and heat of resentment can damage the relationship. Parents often represent the 'old wineskins,' and the 'new wine' of their children's generation tends to stretch the old skins to the breaking point. And the 'new wine' flows where it wills. Frequent communication, and a discernment between what is *wrong,* and that which is only *different,* can be good preventive medicine. In the Seward's case, the 'runaway wine' caused years of heartache and concern. Then the redeeming and restoring God made all things work together for good...

Chapter Twenty-One

Authentic Life

"Their lives have been a symphony of many movements characterizing the delights and struggles of mankind; all full of meaning and emotion. They were just plain instruments. But in the hands of the Master they showed forth His glorious attributes. All the audience was moved. All knew they had been in the presence of greatness."
Reflection of author

If we are not living our lives in tune with the Sermon on the Mount and the Great Commandment (love God and neighbor), then we should step back, go back to square one, and re-orient ourselves. The one thing about real change is - it too seldom happens.

It really isn't all that complicated, although it takes courage and faith to cast all our cares upon Him. It is helpful to remember, "...we are not adequate in ourselves to think anything as coming from ourselves. Our adequacy is in God." (2 Corinthians 3:5)

We give mental assent and make some level of commitment, but are we totally convinced that this is the life we want? Do we want to push our obedience and dying-to-self to this extent? Or, will we be content to rest at a level of living and commitment that will bring approval from our friends? When we do the latter we end up with a "folk Christianity" –one that feels warm and comfortable to all us folks, but may or may not accomplish in and through us what Jesus wants to be and to do.

When the fundamental principles Jesus set forth in the Sermon on the Mount are lived out in our lives through the power of the Holy Spirit, then God can work His will and He is glorified; that is, His attributes shine forth. Otherwise we're just struggling with our own religion...trying harder to get to God in our own strength. Doesn't work!

This is the difference I see in people like Mother Teresa, the Sewards, and a few others, who actually live out an abundance of these truths in their everyday lives. Their fundamental ideology has been transformed by the walk of Jesus, the Word and Spirit of God. It isn't so much the views they articulate, and their manner in doing so, as it is the life they live. They are humble people. Humility is the antithesis of pride. It isn't weakness or mamby-pamby-ness, but is honest and real—not a pretense of being more or less than we really are.

Jesus said, "I desire compassion more than sacrifice."[1] Calvin Miller observes in *Into The Depths of God* that loving Christ and people is not all that easy. "All those who serve Christ and anything else become aware that serving Christ is somewhat easier than loving Christ. As doing is easier than being, serving is easier than loving. In fact, for a great many believers, serving becomes a substitute for loving…serving doesn't make happy Christians, only loving can do that. Serving without loving becomes at last a dull habit that gives us place in the community while it steals our relationship with Christ."

Why is loving so difficult? Because basically it means dying to ourselves, and having an intimate relationship with God in Christ, the fountainhead of love.

Miller also observes, "When we are busy helping other people, it's amazing how unimportant our little grievances can look…even when we are among the hurting, we can arrive at personal peace faster by trying to give understanding to others than by seeking it for ourselves."

When the Sewards were touted as "The Shepherds of the Valley," it was because they had scored high in the eyes of the public in the realms of willingness to help and understand others in any area of need. The community has honored them in a variety of ways over the years, giving testimony to their consistent lifestyle. Talk to those from near and far who have visited their home and the gatherings of the Church (Body of Christ) they've participated in, and the preponderance of feedback will relate to the vitality they found there (i.e., love, warmth, generosity, dependability, hospitality, wise counsel, and down-to-earthedness).

---

1   See Matthew 9:13

The most real thing about the Sewards is that their lives flow from God to people, not the other way around. Their freedom comes from God. Their identity and ministry flow from God. They do not want to do anything that will reflect negatively upon the reputation of God. They struggle to be dependable, to keep all their commitments, and to act out of loving care. Their focus is on people…helping people. That is what consumes them.

I have heard it asked, "Why does Wendell teach on love so much?"

It is because without love, all the other stuff we do is of questionable lasting value. Our motives are suspect. The physical, the flesh, is temporary and passing. True love comes from God and is eternal. Many focus on building lives that will soon fade. Others build upon things of the Spirit that are everlasting. God has made it plain that He values all people. He loves them. Loving others saves us from ourselves…our selfish selves.

This is why the outward look is a key health-producer for us as individuals and collectively for all of Christ's Body, the Church. It keeps us from becoming ingrown and self-centered. The Seward's mission vision is in this vein. Proactive love produces sacrificial acts of service. I believe the world is quick to detect when unconditional love and acceptance are absent in our lives, relationships, and dealings. Jesus clearly makes the point when he says, "…they (the world) will know you are my disciples, if you have love for one another."[2]

Few people will reject God's loving care and compassion in the right clothing. The Sewards experience this on a daily basis. Where there is love there is hope. Faith, hope and love are all vital. They are "God stuff."

And the greatest is love.

Love sees below the surface; love gives value, and it recognizes value in everyone, and heals wounds. The tree-bark of the world, often repulsive, can be thick and ugly, but underneath there is the life reproduction layer, the cambium. The potential for life and growth are there, although obscured to the human eye.

It is the same with the human soul. Like a seed lying dormant for decades in dry soil, under certain conditions of warmth and moisture

---

2 John 13:35

that seed will come alive and grow and reproduce itself thirty, sixty, or a hundredfold. Though buried in the world, once in the presence of love's warmth and the spring of living waters of the Spirit of God, new life is born -- a life which can produce much fruit through generations.

Oftentimes a broken heart becomes a tender heart, an empathetic heart, a compassionate heart, a hungry heart. It doesn't refuse to love because it has been broken…rather, love seeps from its wounds. Wendell and Marilyn have had their hearts broken on several occasions. Satan wanted to knock them down and out. But God, in His infinite mercy and love restored them, giving them strength and wisdom to bear the tragedies. Their response was to trust Him. "Though He slay me, yet will I trust Him." (Job 13:15)

Reflection

Only those who have trusted compasses aligned by God's Spirit and follow His guidance are able to navigate through the stormy seas and treacherous channels of life. Others will do well to join them. And those in the ship of Life can be assured: *the ship won't sink, and the storm won't last forever.* A safe haven is assured.

Jesus didn't bow down to the powers that be even though they kept trying to kill Him. I don't think Jesus today would sit in our pews feeling comfortable and content and agreeing with us that there are others around who are dangerous to our faith, and so we must protect ourselves from them. The problem with Jesus is, He doesn't cater much to our biases and prejudices, or our fears. And He is the Dangerous One. Our self-justification and petty complaining, our finger-pointing and fleshly rationales are in danger when He shows up.

Our minds, even an infinite mind, can produce no higher ideal than Jesus. After all, He is the creator of the entire universe. Everything relates to Him in one way or another. You would think this would remove Him from competition and others would quit, but not so. The enemy lives on…in all of his subtlety and deceit. Whatever and whoever obscures the pre-eminence of Jesus Christ, obscures central, foundational truth and reality, and introduces a false principle of interpretation.

When people like the Sewards come along, depending upon an entirely different arrangement for living than the world or institutional Church, troubles are plentiful. For centuries, mankind has been "killing the apostles and prophets"...those who would speak God's heart and mind into various situations and venues regarding needed correction and guidance. God uses the "humble and contrite heart" to accomplish His work...and hell's gates cannot stand against Him.

Much has been lost of what Jesus originally and continually intends for mankind and for His "Body," the Church. It is as though mankind has been racing down the road of time and has become lost in a cloud of dust generated partly by its own going, and partly from those who don't want others to find the way.

Reflection

The duet of Wendell and Marilyn's lives was one of harmony and purpose. The refrains were many and varied...some sobered by trials, others celebrating victories of redemption and hope.

Chapter Twenty-Two

Decreasing and Increasing

"Faith is not knowing God can,
it is knowing God will."
Ben Stein

After being a Christian for twenty years I was a hard nut to crack. I felt somewhat smug in my own self assurance, convinced that I was close to the cutting edge of what God was doing locally and around the world. But God, knowing me much better than I know myself, for some eternal reason gave me a relationship with the Sewards. It took several years of spending time together, weekly meetings, and observing their walk in the world, before I experienced any significant transformation in my own life. I could pretty well talk the talk, but walking the walk requires a lot of overcoming: habits, traditions, confusion, selfishness and pride (the greatest "unfinished task"), ignorance, wrong perspectives.

And the longer I think about it, the longer the list gets. I have kind of a sneaky feeling there are many people like me, who study the Bible, pray regularly, and make a concerted effort to do what the Bible says …and have the whole shooting match completely backward from how God has designed us to function.

In researching this book, we ran into the same thing over and over again: "I don't know how they do it! They go night and day. They always seem to appear where people are hurting or needy, whether it's night or day. Their home is inundated with people and they just think it is great. They seem to take no thought of themselves. Marilyn has providential wisdom. Wendell has grace 'til the cows come home." …and more.

Yes, at times they do seem super-natural. Doing above and beyond what most do. Who can live like that? Who can at times seem omnipresent, and at others omnipotent, and still others omniscient? Yet, at the same time they have encountered a number of traumatic trials, many within their own family. Some of these, by their own admission, were compounded and complicated by their own attitudes and blindness.

They have been disappointed by others, yet they feel they may not have had reasonable expectation levels, and at times may have had blinders on that didn't let them see or detect the warning signals. They agonized and struggled from within and without. They had many sleepless nights. Over the decades they grew significantly, shedding early beliefs and convictions as they were replaced by new insights, truths, revelations, experiences.

Wendell and Marilyn have discovered the truth of, "To have the heart and mind of Christ, I must *decrease* and He must *increase*."[1] They have desired for their fundamental attitude to be one of humility and surrender. Surrendering and dying do not come easy. And it takes faith that God is who He says He is. That truly He alone has the words of life—for He is life!

Repeated decisions based upon unselfish love, depending upon God for His wisdom and power, have gradually produced habits that align, or are coming into alignment, with the righteousness of God. Old habits and cultural mores aren't shed easily, but even when they are, caution is needed lest we find ourselves doing things by rote instead of being energized by God's Spirit. Brother Lawrence[2] said he "practiced the presence of God." We could all benefit in doing that.

Reflection

God will show up to represent Himself and fill His disciple with His Holy Spirit when the disciple craves an intimate relationship; when his or her adoration and worship are wholehearted. Miracles (happenings we can't explain or figure out how happen) will become more commonplace. The "original design" personality that has been obscured by the consequences of 'The Fall', will emerge and blossom.

---

1   John 3:30

2   Brother Lawrence, *Practice of The Presence of God: Best Rule of a Holy Life*, (London, Epworth Press, 168X) Born in France in about 1610, Brother Lawrence was known for his humility and personal walk with God. His "writings" were really recorded interviews by a person designated by the cardinal who was impressed by Brother Andrew's holiness.

Unconditional and indiscriminate love and acceptance...I wasn't doing very well in this department, especially the *unconditional* part. But I was beginning to come to the understanding that everyone has value. Meeting weekly with the Sewards, I certainly would have been without excuse on this one. I never saw anyone really turn Wendell off or rumple his feathers, except, like Jesus, those who were supposed to be, or claimed to be, representing God but were leading people astray. Even then he would never condemn them.

Growing in this area little by little, I began to see changes in my family, in my relationships around the world, in our own neighborhood and valley. Our circle of close friends expanded to include many non-churchgoers and neighbors. I was surprised when neighbor's kids began asking if I would "do" their marriages, a very profound privilege...and a very profound surprise.

I was also surprised when one dear non-church friend, asked me to do his wife's funeral... then three years later his own. Another called to tell me how Jesus had become real to him, actually sitting with him and telling him of His love. "Bob...He has a place for me and this is the greatest moment! He was here. He sat right there!"

That evening my dear friend slipped excitedly into Jesus' presence. It is amazing, absolutely amazing, where loving care will flow. It's never too late!

This is all to say, there are rivers of influence and change streaming from the Sewards' lives which are spawning life far and wide, even beyond our knowledge, and which will continue to do so through generations to come. When anyone really puts Jesus' principles into shoe-leather, there really will be eternal results. There will be transformation in individuals and in society. I'm afraid many of us who call ourselves "Christian" today are only nibbling at the edges of the abundant, obedient life.

Tragedies, as personal and as present as they were, did not produce bitterness and doom. Instead, Wendell and Marilyn were found in seats of reflection tenderized to a new level of sensitivity and understanding. Much of their lives held hidden meaning. The most profound impact is often the result of pure, unsullied motives and attitudes that are puzzling to the intellectual and the suspicious, in terms of how simple living, fundamental hospitality, frugal surroundings, gentle and polite mannerisms, generosity, and a servant's heart, can touch so many lives in a transformational way.

The Sewards knew about forgiveness and its awesome power for breaking the bonds of the past, and in restoring relationships. Unbeknownst to most, they forgave at least forty-thousand dollars of a loan made to the Berean church at the time of the construction of the new church building. They did this two years after being removed from the church. This is significant indicator of the victory which they realized after one of the greatest trials of their lives.

Wendell as a young boy, never strongly assertive, matured into a gentleman of patience, generosity, and love. Marilyn as a young girl, sometimes separated from others by her capableness and convictions, mellowed into a vessel of leadership and compassion.

The real meaning of life is fundamental. Love in action. *"Love the Lord your god with all your heart, all your soul and all your mind, and your neighbor as yourself!"* *"The greatest of these is love."*

Reflection

When we become sons and daughters of God there is an awareness deep within our souls. No matter what manner of persons we are, we become overcome by a fondness, a tenderness, a graciousness, a kindness that beggars description. The further we travel life's path the more indelible they become in our character. They find expression in multiplied acts of selflessness. Such is the portion of the Sewards.

Chapter Twenty-Three

The Greatest is Love

"Faith, hope and love remain...
The greatest of these is love."
1Corinthians 13:13

Jesus' life was and is down-to-earth. His life on this planet was powerfully transforming, continually astonishing and wonderfully refreshing. Amidst all of the awesomeness of his stories, teachings, and healings, there was great hope and joy. Life was exciting and adventurous, filled with meaning and purpose. Miracles of healing and power combined with loving acceptance had massive impact. People couldn't get enough of Jesus. If they couldn't be near him, they at least wanted to hear the stories from those who were...what he had done last week, yesterday, this morning.

It was unbelievable. He would leave the adoring crowds to take a side path where there would be a leper, or prostitute, or some other disenfranchised person whose station or status in life told them they were worthless. He wanted them to know he valued them greatly. His love and acceptance, His words and healing convinced them.

The crowds would stand in awe as the leaders of the Jews would try to trap Jesus, yet end up embarrassing themselves. He disclosed their intentions and put his finger on their deceit. The people would declare, "Who is this man? He can feed the hungry, heal the sick, calm the seas, make my heart burn within me, and stand against the religious leaders!"

And then they couldn't find Him. He had taken some time aside to pray...to fellowship with His Father, to rest, and to contemplate. When nations lift Him up He prospers them, and people live in harmony. When they trample on Him and His ideals, they suffer the consequences and end up without hope and without true meaning.

Don't you wish He were here among us now? These days? He would be encouraging the down-hearted, healing the sick and the confused, feeding the hungry, setting the captive free, and standing against religious leaders who mislead his sheep. He is here...and He is doing this, but in limited measure. He finds so few willing bodies who really understand His heart and are galvanized by His love; so few who are not trapped in religious church systems or subverted by the promises of position, passion and possession, the big guns of the enemy of man's soul.

There are a few who have not sold their birthright for a mess of pottage.

In three and a half years, Jesus, through his walk and his words, communicated a revolutionary new standard for living. He provided fundamental principles for Kingdom living, producing broad areas of purposeful and meaningful life here on this planet. The Sermon on the Mount includes them directly and indirectly. Summarized, the core of these basic *touchstones* for living are:

☞ Unconditional love—compassion, grace, forgiveness, and acceptance
☞ Humility and servanthood and dependability
☞ Hospitality and generosity
☞ Equality and unity
☞ The search for and salvation of the lost

A challenging exercise is to compare your (my) life with these touchstones Jesus set forth. It is the truth and power of these principles being lived out in the Sewards' lives that drew Judi and me and hundreds of others to them and to a closer walk with Jesus. I am convinced I know how some of those people in Galilee felt when Jesus moved among them. Their hearts were searching for purpose and meaning, as are all hearts in all time, and their hearts were warmed by His presence, and galvanized by his expressions of love.

We have been created with the need and desire for love and acceptance, for hope and security, for giving and receiving, for reproduction. When these attributes are within our reach and we begin to experience them in unsullied fashion, our hearts do burn within us.

Eugene Peterson in *The Message* captures the essence of this in his overview preceding Chapter One of Colossians: "Hardly anyone who hears the true story of Jesus and learns the facts of his true life and teaching, crucifixion and resurrection, walks away with a shrug of the shoulders, dismissing him as unimportant. People ignorant of the story or misinformed about it, of course, regularly dismiss him. But with few exceptions, the others know instinctively that they are dealing with a most remarkable greatness."

The foundational principles Jesus set forth are not just good intellectual ideas or opinions, they are the very substance of eternal life in the Kingdom of God. They are what we were created for. Only one person can live them without any hypocrisy and that person is Jesus Christ. When Paul says, "Christ in you is your only hope of glory," this is what he had in mind.

When he says, "I am crucified with Christ; and it is no longer I who live, but Christ lives in me; the life I now live in the flesh I live by faith in the Son of God who loved me and gave Himself up for me,"[1] this is what he is talking about.

The Holy Spirit, the very spirit of Christ the Creator, is the only person who can live this life in and through us, and it is our responsibility to align our human spirit and our wills with His Spirit. It isn't enough for us to try to live this way and then gradually we'll believe it. Our hypocrisy is already showing all over the place in this regard. Jesus saw right through this with the Pharisees, and He sees right through it with us.

Can this be lived today…here and now? Yes, that is primarily what this book is about -- two lives, dying to self, and living for God…allowing and inviting Him to live through them. The Sewards aren't perfect or perfected yet, but we do see this life in them, and, thankfully, in a growing number of people. Their fundamental ideology and lifestyle have been transformed by the Word and Spirit of God. They comprehend and participate in Jesus' fundamental principles of life.

Jesus wants to walk the countrysides and the city streets today just as He did two thousand years ago. You and I, like Wendell and Marilyn, can make that possible …maybe not perfectly, but certainly possible.

Reflection

There are some men and women who change the nature of history for the better just through the lives they live. These give living testimony

---

1   Galatians 2:20

to the fundamental truths and promises of God and His Word. Many, perhaps most, are dressed in every day garb and those who know them may or may not know the influence they are having on society. This was the portion of Wendell and Marilyn Seward: *Shepherds of Love*!

---The End---

After Word

Wendell announced on Oct 20, 2007 at Grace Community that he had terminal cancer, with the prognosis of going to be with his Lord in the next few months. On the afternoon of the twentieth of December, two months later, Wendell made his exodus from time into eternity. He was surrounded by a few family members and friends. He taught us how to live, and how to die.

Marilyn has carried on marvelously, although she has had her moments. She fights loneliness at times, then immediately focuses on those needing help, especially a group of about fifteen women who are all coming off drugs, finding themselves in all kinds of snarls and releases. Wendell had been meeting one of the girls in jail, and after his death, 'Lisa' called Marilyn and wanted to talk to her about the Lord. She became a Christian and began influencing her friends, bringing them one by one to Marilyn. Many have become believers, some end up going back to jail, or reverting to alcohol and drugs, and although it has been 'three steps forward, two steps back' they are all making progress. Marilyn shares, "Never would I have dreamed that I would love these girls so much or that they would consume so much of my life."

Marilyn is still involved in the community and was recently re-elected to the Etna City Council. Her home remains a haven for many needy persons. She is leading the group at Grace Community Church every Sunday, as did Wendell and Mike and Karla Yaconelli before her. The love of God and one another continues as the theme in word and deed. Respect and admiration for her and Wendell remain "domiciled in a thousand hearts."

About the author

Bob Waymire, for the past nearly twenty-two years has lived in Etna, California in the Northern California mountains. During these years, he and his wife, Judi, met *weekly* with Wendell (deceased Dec. 2007) and Marilyn Seward for breakfast at a local restaurant.

Bob was born and raised in Southern Nevada. He served in the Naval Air during the Korean War. Afterward he worked as a systems engineer in aerospace at Lockheed Missile in Sunnyvale, California. He then bought a cattle ranch in the mountains of Colorado near Rifle. After suffering through a divorce he returned to aerospace as a program consultant.

Three years later, in 1969, he had a life changing (spiritual) experience, and two years later married Judi Holt. Beginning in 1973 he went into full-time missions devoted mainly to mission's strategy and research worldwide. His travels have taken him to sixty-five countries. Bob founded Global Mapping International in 1983, and LIGHT International in 1991 to assist in the informational aspects of world missions.

He has published several research and strategy related manuals, and co-authored, *Discovering Your City: Bringing Light to the Task of Community Transformation, (2000, LIGHT International).*

Having written award winning poetry, he continues writing today in a variety of genre, and continues to serve in a consultive role for world missions.

Bob and Judi currently live in Etna, California.